DISMANTLING THE EMPIRE

DISMANTLING THE EMPIRE

AMERICA'S LAST BEST HOPE

CHALMERS JOHNSON

METROPOLITAN BOOKS HENRY HOLT AND COMPANY NEW YORK

Metropolitan Books
Henry Holt and Company, LLC
Publishers since 1866
175 Fifth Avenue
New York, New York 10010
www.henryholt.com

Metropolitan Books® and m® are registered trademarks of
Henry Holt and Company, LLC.

The chapter "Blowback World" first appeared in slightly altered form in the *London Review of Books* in the October 21, 2004, issue (vol. 26, no. 20), pp. 25–28.

"America's Unwelcome Advances" first appeared August 22, 2008,
on MotherJones.com and is used in this book with its permission.
Copyright © 2008 by the Foundation for National Progress.

All other pieces, except the introduction, first appeared on the website TomDispatch.com.

Library of Congress Cataloging-in-Publication Data
Johnson, Chalmers.
  Dismantling the empire : America's last best hope / Chalmers Johnson.—1st ed.
    p. cm.
  Includes index.
  ISBN 978-0-8050-9303-2
  1. United States—Foreign relations—1989– 2. United States—Military
policy. 3. United States. Dept. of Defense—Appropriations and expenditures.
4. Intervention (International law) 5. Imperialism. I. Title.
  E840.J6325 2010
  973.92—dc22   2010003167

First Edition 2010

Designed by Kelly S. Too

Printed in the United States of America
1 3 5 7 9 10 8 6 4 2

CONTENTS

DISMANTLING THE EMPIRE

THE SUICIDE OPTION

During the last years of the Clinton administration I was in my mid-sixties, retired from teaching Asian international relations at the University of California and deeply bored by my specialty, Japanese politics. It seemed that Japan would continue forever as a docile satellite of the United States, a safe place to park tens of thousands of American troops, as well as ships and aircraft, all ready to assert American hegemony over the entire Pacific region. I was then in the process of rethinking my research and determining where I should go next.

At the time, one aspect of the Clinton administration especially worried me. In the aftermath of the breakup and disappearance of the Soviet Union, U.S. officials seemed unbearably complacent about America's global ascendancy. They were visibly bathed in a glow of post–Cold War triumphalism. It was hard to avoid their high-decibel assertions that our country was "unique" in history, their insistence that we were now, and for the imaginable future, the "lone superpower" or, in the words of Secretary of State Madeleine Albright, "the indispensable nation." The implication was that we would be so for an eternity. If ever there was a self-satisfied country that seemed headed for a rude awakening, it was the United States.

I became concerned as well that we were taking for granted the goodwill of so many nations, even as we incautiously ran up a tab of insults to the rest of the world. What I couldn't quite imagine was that President Clinton's arrogance and his administration's risk taking—the 1998 cruise missile attack on the al-Shifa pharmaceutical plant in Khartoum, Sudan, for instance, or the 1999 bombing of the Chinese embassy in Belgrade, Serbia, during the Kosovo war—might presage an existential crisis for the nation. Our stance toward the rest of the world certainly seemed reckless to me, but not in itself of overwhelming significance. We were, after all, the world's richest nation, even if we were delusional in assuming that our wealth would be a permanent condition. We were also finally at peace (more or less) after a long period, covering much of the twentieth century, in which we had been engaged in costly, deadly wars.

As I quietly began to worry, it crossed my mind that we in the United States had long taken all of Asia for granted, despite the fact that we had fought three wars there, only one of which we had won. My fears grew that the imperial tab we were running up would come due sooner than any of us had expected, and that payment might be sought in ways both unexpected and deeply unnerving. In this mood, I began to write a book of analysis that was also meant as a warning, and for a title I drew on a term of CIA tradecraft. I called it *Blowback*.

The book's reception on publication in 2000 might serve as a reasonable gauge of the overconfident mood of the country. It was generally ignored and, where noted and commented upon, rejected as the oddball thoughts of a formerly eminent Japan specialist. I was therefore less shocked than most when, as the Clinton years ended, we Americans made a serious mistake that helped turn what passed for fringe prophecy into stark reality. We let George W. Bush take the White House.

He was a man superficially well enough qualified to be president. The governor of a populous state, he had also been the recipient of one of the best—or, in any case, most expensive—educations available to an American. Yale College and Harvard Business School might have seemed like a guarantee against a sophomoric ignoramus occupying the highest office in the land, but contrary to most expectations that was precisely what we got. The American public did not actually elect him, of course. He was, in the end, appointed to the highest office in the land by a conservative cabal of Supreme Court justices in what certainly qualified as one of the most bizarre moments in the history of American politics.

During his eight reckless years as president, Bush, his vice president Dick Cheney, his secretary of defense Donald Rumsfeld, and the other neoconservative and right-wing officials he appointed, war-lovers all, drove the country as close to the precipice as was humanly possible. After the attacks of 9/11, he would have been wise to treat al-Qaeda as the criminal organization it was. Instead, he launched two wars of aggression in close succession against Iraq and Afghanistan. The irony was that had he done absolutely nothing, the political situations in both countries would likely have resolved themselves, given time, in ways tolerable for us and our allies based on the constellation of forces at work in each place. Instead, his policies entrenched Shia Muslims in Iraq, repeated all the mistakes of other foreign invaders—particularly the British and more recently the Russians—in Afghanistan, and enhanced the power of Iran in the Persian Gulf region.

As a result of his ill-informed and bungling strategic moves, President Bush left our armed forces seriously depleted, with worn-out equipment, badly misused human resources, and staggering medical (and thus financial) obligations to thousands of young Americans suffering from disabling wounds, including those inflicted on their minds. Meanwhile, our high command, which went into Afghanistan and Iraq stuck in the land war doctrines of World War II but filled with dreamy, high-tech, "netcentric" fantasies, is now mired in the failed counterinsurgency doctrine of the Vietnam era. That's what evidently passes for progress in the Pentagon these days. Its officials still have hardly a clue as to how to deal with nonstate actors like al-Qaeda.

At the same time, the Bush administration paved the way for, and then presided over, a close to catastrophic economic and financial collapse that skirted national and international insolvency. Fueled by huge tax cuts for the wealthiest Americans, profligate spending on two wars (as well as future wars and the weaponry to fight them), the appointment of Republican ideologues to critical positions of trust, and accounting and management practices that exacerbated just about every other problem, the Bush administration plunged us into the worst financial crisis since the Great Depression.

As if these failures weren't bad enough, during Bush's tenure the armed forces were authorized to torture Muslims captured virtually anywhere on earth; the Department of Justice turned a blind eye to the clandestine electronic surveillance of the general public; and the Central Intelligence Agency was given carte blanche to kidnap terror suspects in other countries and transfer them to regimes where they could be interrogated under torture, as well as to assassinate supposed terror suspects just about anywhere on the planet. From Afghanistan and Iraq to Lithuania, Thailand, and Guantánamo Bay, Cuba, the United States set up an offshore system of (in)justice, including "black sites" (secret CIA prisons) that put many of its most outrageous acts beyond oversight or the reach of the law—any law. In the meantime, the United States also withdrew from many important international treaties, including the one banning the production of antiballistic missiles.

The history books will certainly record that George W. Bush was likely the single worst president in the history of the American republic. Nonetheless, they will also point out that he merely accelerated trends long under way, particularly our devotion to militarism and our dependence on the military-industrial complex.

In 2008, faced with a truly dysfunctional government, the American people unexpectedly demonstrated that they got the message. The presidential candidacy of Barack Obama reignited a long-dormant idealism, particularly among those who believed, on the basis of their own lives, that the political system had been rigged against them. The national outpouring of enthusiasm for this African American presidential candidate led many around the world to believe that the American people were ready to abandon their infatuation with imperialism. They assumed that we were exhibiting a desire for genuine reform before the trends of the Clinton-Bush years became irreversible.

During his campaign Barack Obama promised to close our extrajudicial detention camp at Guantánamo Bay; restore legally sanctioned practices, particularly within the Department of Justice; provide nearly all citizens with health insurance and other life support systems that are routine in most advanced industrial democracies; take global warming seriously; and implement any number of laws that were being honored only in the breach, including those protecting personal privacy. Obama's proposed reform program was massive, long overdue, and popularly welcomed.

Conspicuously absent from this lengthy agenda, however, was one significant sector of American life. Only those of us who had long watched this area noted Obama's silence and were alarmed for what it suggested about his future presidency. This omission concerned the massive apparatus that enables what I have called our global "empire of bases" to exist and function. In the campaign, he said little about the armed forces (other than that he would like to expand the Army and Marines), the military-industrial complex, the Pentagon's failure to account properly for the vast sums it spends, the growing clandestine role of our proliferating intelligence services, or the subcontracting of extremely sensitive national security tasks to the private sector.

Given the degree to which, as this book emphasizes, the Pentagon and the powerful forces that surround it have played such a crucial role in leading this country to the edge, this campaign omission was anything but auspicious. It is undoubtedly true that a presidential candidate determined to take on these forces might have had a difficult time cutting the Pentagon, the "intelligence community," and the military-industrial complex down to size. Unfortunately, Obama did not even try. The evidence already suggests that huge vested interests in the status quo blocked this president from the start—and, no less important, that when it came to our national security state and our global imperial presence he acquiesced.

I have written elsewhere that on his first day in office every president is given a highly secret briefing about the clandestine powers at his disposal and that no president has ever failed to use them. It is increasingly clear that while pursuing his agenda in other areas, Obama, who made James Jones, a retired Marine Corps commandant, the head of his National Security Council and Robert Gates, a former Cold War CIA director and holdover from the Bush years, his secretary of defense, is going along with what the militarist establishment in Washington recommends, while offering little in the way of resistance. As commander in chief, he must be supportive of our armed forces, but nothing obliges him to take pride in American imperialism or to "finish the job" that George Bush began in Afghanistan, as he seems intent on doing.

The essays in this volume were, for the most part, written over the last three years. Although some look back at the recent past, most focus on our limited resources for continuing to behave like an empire and what the likely outcome will be. We are not, of course, the first country to face the choice between republic and empire, nor the first to have our imperial dreams stretch our means to the breaking point and threaten our future. But this book suggests that among the alternatives available to us as a nation, we are choosing what I call the suicide option. It also suggests that it might not have to be this way, that we still could move in a different direction.

We could begin to dismantle our empire of bases. We could, to offer but one example, simply close Futenma, the enormous Marine Corps base on Okinawa much disliked by the new Japanese government that took office in Japan in 2009. Instead, we continue to try to browbeat the Japanese into acting as our docile satellite by forcing them to pay for the transfer of our Marines either to the island of Guam (which can't support such a base either) or to an environmentally sensitive area elsewhere on Okinawa.

Seldom has an incoming president been given greater benefit of the doubt than President-elect Obama. When, for no apparent good reason, he decided to retain President Bush's top military appointment in our war zones, CENTCOM commander General David Petraeus, hang on to Secretary of Defense Gates, and later reinforce the large American expeditionary force already fighting in Afghanistan, Republicans spoke of continuity and some Democrats explained it as a brilliant ploy to shift blame for an all but certain American defeat to Republican holdovers. But Obama certainly had other options. For secretary of defense he might have turned to someone like retired Army lieutenant colonel Andrew Bacevich, author of the best-selling book *The Limits of Power*. Nor were generals Petraeus and Afghan war commander Stanley

McChrystal, who had previously run counterterror operations for Bush in both Iraq and Afghanistan, inevitable choices. But these were the people Obama appointed. They, in turn, have devised policies that have allowed him to continue the war in Afghanistan in the face of grave public doubts, just as they did in Iraq for Obama's predecessor.

Whether or not becoming a war president is what Obama truly intended, the greatest obstacle to his war policies is that the United States cannot afford them. The federal deficit was already spiraling out of control before the Great Recession of 2008. Since then, the government has only gone more deeply into debt to prevent the collapse of critical financial institutions as well as the housing industry. It is not clear that Obama's measures to overcome the Great Recession will do anything more than take resources away from necessary projects and leave the country that much closer to bankruptcy. It is absolutely certain that the estimated trillion dollars a year spent on the defense establishment will make it almost impossible for the United States to avoid the ultimate limit on imperialism: overstretch and insolvency.

In December 2009, the United States had its best and perhaps last chance to avoid the suicide option. After a three-month review of our activities in Afghanistan, when he might have found a way to disengage, Obama instead decided to escalate—at a cost he estimated, in a speech at West Point explaining his decision, at $30 billion per year but certain to go far higher, not to mention the costs in human lives—American, allied, and Afghan. Although by then a majority of our population believed we had done everything we could for a poor central Asian country led by a hopelessly corrupt government, President Obama chose to continue our imperialist project. As Hamlet said, "It is not, nor it cannot come to good."

None of this was inevitable, although it may have been unavoidable given the hubris and arrogance of our national leadership.

PART I

WHAT WE DID

1

BLOWBACK WORLD

November 5, 2004

Steve Coll ends his important book on Afghanistan, *Ghost Wars: The Secret History of the CIA*, by quoting Afghan president Hamid Karzai: "What an unlucky country." Americans might find this a convenient way to ignore what their government did in Afghanistan between 1979 and the present, but luck had nothing to do with it. Brutal, incompetent, secret operations of the U.S. Central Intelligence Agency, frequently manipulated by the military intelligence agencies of Pakistan and Saudi Arabia, caused the catastrophic devastation of this poor country. On the evidence contained in Coll's book, neither the Americans nor their victims in numerous Muslim and Third World countries will ever know peace until the Central Intelligence Agency has been abolished.

It should by now be generally accepted that the Soviet invasion of Afghanistan on Christmas Eve 1979 was deliberately provoked by the United States. In his memoir published in 1996, the former CIA director Robert Gates made it clear that the American intelligence services began to aid the mujahideen guerrillas not after the Soviet invasion, but six months before it. In an interview two years later with *Le Nouvel Observateur*, President Carter's national security adviser Zbigniew Brzezinski proudly confirmed Gates's assertion. "According to the official version of history," Brzezinski said, "CIA aid to the mujahideen began during 1980, that's to say, after the Soviet army invaded Afghanistan. But the reality, kept secret until now, is completely different: on 3 July 1979 President Carter signed the first directive for secret aid to the opponents of the pro-Soviet regime in Kabul. And on the same day, I wrote a note to the president in which I explained that in my opinion this aid would lead to a Soviet military intervention."

Asked whether he in any way regretted these actions, Brzezinski replied: "Regret what? The secret operation was an excellent idea. It drew the Russians into the Afghan trap and you want me to regret it? On the day that the Soviets officially crossed the border, I wrote to President Carter, saying, in essence: 'We now have the opportunity of giving to the USSR its Vietnam War.'"

NOUVEL OBSERVATEUR: And neither do you regret having supported Islamic fundamentalism, which has given arms and advice to future terrorists?

BRZEZINSKI: What is more important in world history? The Taliban or the collapse of the Soviet empire? Some agitated Muslims or the liberation of Central Europe and the end of the Cold War?

Even though the demise of the Soviet Union owes more to Mikhail Gorbachev than to Afghanistan's partisans, Brzezinski certainly helped produce "agitated Muslims," and the consequences have been obvious ever since. Carter, Brzezinski, and their successors in the Reagan and first Bush administrations, including Gates, Dick Cheney, Donald Rumsfeld, Condoleezza Rice, Paul Wolfowitz, Richard Armitage, and Colin Powell, all bear some responsibility for the 1.8 million Afghan casualties, 2.6 million refugees, and 10 million unexploded land mines that followed from their decisions. They must also share the blame for the blowback that struck New York and Washington on September 11, 2001. After all, al-Qaeda was an organization they helped create and arm.

A WIND BLOWS IN FROM AFGHANISTAN

The term "blowback" first appeared in a classified CIA postaction report on the overthrow of the Iranian government in 1953, carried out in the interests of British Petroleum. In 2000, James Risen of the *New York Times* explained:

> When the Central Intelligence Agency helped overthrow Muhammad Mossadegh as Iran's prime minister in 1953, ensuring another 25 years of rule for Shah Mohammad Reza Pahlavi, the CIA was already figuring that its first effort to topple a foreign government would not be its last. The CIA, then just six years old and deeply committed to winning the Cold War, viewed its covert action in Iran as a blueprint for coup plots elsewhere around the world, and so commissioned a secret history to detail for future generations of CIA operatives how it had been done. . . . Amid the sometimes curious argot of the spy world—"safebases" and "assets" and the like—the CIA warns of the possibilities of "blowback." The word . . . has since come into use as shorthand for the unintended consequences of covert operations.

"Blowback" does not refer simply to reactions to historical events, but more specifically to reactions to operations carried out by the U.S. government that are kept secret from the American public and from most of their representatives in Congress. This means that when civilians become victims of a retaliatory strike, they are at first unable to put it in context or to understand the sequence of events that led up to it. Even though the American people may not know what has been done in their name, those on the receiving end certainly do: they include the people of Iran (1953), Guatemala (1954), Cuba (1959 to the present), Congo (1960), Brazil (1964), Indonesia (1965), Vietnam (1961–73), Laos (1961–73), Cambodia (1969–73), Greece (1967–73), Chile (1973), Afghanistan (1979 to the present), El Salvador, Guatemala and Nicaragua (1980s), and Iraq (1991 to the present). Not surprisingly, sometimes these victims try to get even.

There is a direct line between the attacks on September 11, 2001—the most significant instance of blowback in the history of the CIA—and the events of 1979. In that year, revolutionaries threw both the shah and the Americans out of Iran, and the CIA, with full presidential authority, began its largest ever clandestine operation: the secret arming of Afghan freedom fighters to wage a proxy war against the Soviet Union, which involved the recruitment and training of militants from all over the Islamic world. Steve Coll's book is a classic study of blowback and is a better, fuller reconstruction of this history than the *Final Report of the National Commission on Terrorist Attacks upon the United States* (the "9/11 Commission Report").

From 1989 to 1992, Coll was the *Washington Post*'s South Asia bureau chief, based in New Delhi. Given the CIA's paranoid and often self-defeating secrecy, what makes his book especially interesting is how he came to know what he claims to know. He has read everything on the Afghan insurgency and the civil wars that followed, and he has been given access to the original manuscript of Robert Gates's memoir (Gates was the CIA director from 1991 to 1993), but his main source is some two hundred interviews conducted between the autumn of 2001 and the summer of 2003 with numerous CIA officials as well as politicians, military officers, and spies from all the countries involved except Russia. He identifies CIA officials only if their names have already been made public. Many of his most important interviews were on the record, and he quotes from them extensively.

Among the notable figures who agreed to be interviewed were Benazir Bhutto, who was candid about having lied to American officials for two years about Pakistan's aid to the Taliban, and Anthony Lake, the U.S. national security adviser from 1993 to 1997, who let it be known that he thought CIA director James Woolsey was "arrogant, tin-eared and brittle." Woolsey was so disliked by Clinton that when an apparent suicide pilot crashed a single-engine Cessna airplane on the south lawn of the White House in 1994, jokers suggested it might be the CIA director trying to get an appointment with the president.

Among the CIA people who talked to Coll are Gates; Woolsey; Howard Hart, Islamabad station chief in 1981; Clair George, former head of clandestine operations; William Piekney, Islamabad station chief from 1984 to 1986; Cofer Black, Khartoum station chief in the mid-1990s and director of the Counterterrorist Center from 1999 to 2002; Fred Hitz, a former CIA inspector general; Thomas Twetten, deputy director of operations, 1991–93; Milton Bearden, chief of station at Islamabad, 1986–89; Duane R. "Dewey" Clarridge, head of the Counterterrorist Center from 1986 to 1988; Vincent Cannistraro, an officer in the Counterterrorist Center shortly after it was opened in 1986; and an official Coll identifies only as "Mike," the head of the "bin Laden Unit" within the Counterterrorist Center from 1997 to 1999, who was subsequently revealed to be Michael F. Scheuer, the anonymous author of *Imperial Hubris: Why the West Is Losing the War on Terror.*

In 1973, General Sardar Mohammed Daoud, the cousin and brother-in-law of King Zahir Shah, overthrew the king, declared Afghanistan a republic, and instituted a program of modernization. Zahir Shah went into exile in Rome. These developments made possible the rise of the People's Democratic Party of Afghanistan, a pro-Soviet communist party, which, in early 1978, with extensive help from the USSR, overthrew President Daoud. The communists' policies of secularization in turn provoked a violent response from devout Islamists. The anticommunist revolt that began at Herat in western Afghanistan in March 1979 originated in a government initiative to teach girls to read. The fundamentalist Afghans opposed to this were supported by a triumvirate of nations—the United States, Pakistan, and Saudi Arabia—with quite diverse motives, but the United States didn't take these differences seriously until it was too late. By the time the Americans woke up, at the end of the 1990s, the radical Islamist Taliban had established its government in Kabul. Recognized only by Pakistan, Saudi Arabia, and the United Arab Emirates, it granted Osama bin Laden freedom of action and offered him protection from American efforts to capture or kill him.

Coll concludes:

> The Afghan government that the United States eventually chose to support beginning in the late autumn of 2001—a federation of Ahmed Shah Massoud's organization [the Northern warlords], exiled intellectuals and royalist Pashtuns—was available for sponsorship a decade before, but the United States could not see a reason then to challenge the alternative, radical Islamist vision promoted by Pakistani and Saudi intelligence. . . . Indif-

ference, lassitude, blindness, paralysis and commercial greed too often shaped American foreign policy in Afghanistan and South Asia during the 1990s.

FUNDING THE FUNDAMENTALISTS

The motives of the White House and the CIA were shaped by the Cold War: a determination to kill as many Soviet soldiers as possible and the desire to restore some aura of rugged machismo as well as credibility that U.S. leaders feared they had lost when the shah of Iran was overthrown. The CIA had no intricate strategy for the war it was unleashing in Afghanistan. Howard Hart, the agency's representative in the Pakistani capital, told Coll that he understood his orders as "You're a young man; here's your bag of money, go raise hell. Don't fuck it up, just go out there and kill Soviets." These orders came from a most peculiar American. William Casey, the CIA's director from January 1981 to January 1987, was a Catholic Knight of Malta educated by Jesuits. Statues of the Virgin Mary filled his mansion, called Maryknoll, on Long Island. He attended mass daily and urged Christianity on anyone who asked his advice. Once settled as CIA director under Reagan, he began to funnel covert action funds through the Catholic Church to anticommunists in Poland and Central America, sometimes in violation of American law. He believed fervently that by increasing the Catholic Church's reach and power he could contain communism's advance, or reverse it. From Casey's convictions grew the most important U.S. foreign policies of the 1980s: support for an international anti-Soviet crusade in Afghanistan and sponsorship of state terrorism in Nicaragua, El Salvador, and Guatemala.

Casey knew next to nothing about Islamic fundamentalism or the grievances of Middle Eastern nations against Western imperialism. He saw political Islam and the Catholic Church as natural allies in the counterstrategy of covert action to thwart Soviet imperialism. He believed that the USSR was trying to strike at the United States in Central America and in the oil-producing states of the Middle East. He supported Islam as a counter to the Soviet Union's atheism, and Coll suggests that he sometimes conflated lay Catholic organizations such as Opus Dei with the Muslim Brotherhood, the Egyptian extremist organization, of which Ayman al-Zawahiri, Osama bin Laden's chief lieutenant, was a passionate member. The Muslim Brotherhood's branch in Pakistan, the Jamaat-e-Islami, was strongly backed by the Pakistani army, and Coll writes that Casey, more than any other American, was responsible for welding the alliance of the CIA, Saudi intelligence, and the army of General Mohammed Zia-ul-Haq, Pakistan's military dictator from 1977 to 1988. On the suggestion of the Pakistani Inter-Services Intelligence (ISI) organization, Casey went so far as to print thousands of copies of the Koran, which he shipped to the Afghan frontier for distribution in Afghanistan and Soviet Uzbekistan. He also fomented, without presidential authority, Muslim attacks inside the USSR and always held that the CIA's clandestine officers were too timid. He preferred the type represented by his friend Oliver North.

Over time, Casey's position hardened into CIA dogma, which its agents, protected by secrecy from ever having their ignorance exposed, enforced in every way they could. The agency resolutely refused to help choose winners and losers among the Afghan jihad's guerrilla leaders. The result, according to Coll, was that "Zia-ul-Haq's political and religious agenda in Afghanistan gradually became the CIA's own." In the era after Casey, some scholars, journalists, and members of Congress questioned the agency's lavish support of the Pakistan-backed Islamist general Gulbuddin Hekmatyar, especially after he refused to shake hands with

Ronald Reagan because he was an infidel. But Milton Bearden, the Islamabad station chief from 1986 to 1989, and Frank Anderson, chief of the Afghan task force at Langley, vehemently defended Hekmatyar on the grounds that "he fielded the most effective anti-Soviet fighters."

Even after the Soviet Union withdrew from Afghanistan in 1988, the CIA continued to follow Pakistani initiatives, such as aiding Hekmatyar's successor, Mullah Omar, the leader of the Taliban. When Edmund McWilliams, the State Department's special envoy to the Afghan resistance in 1988–89, wrote that "American authority and billions of dollars in taxpayer funding had been hijacked at the war's end by a ruthless anti-American cabal of Islamists and Pakistani intelligence officers determined to impose their will on Afghanistan," CIA officials denounced him and planted stories in the embassy that he might be homosexual or an alcoholic. Meanwhile, Afghanistan descended into one of the most horrific civil wars of the twentieth century. The CIA never fully corrected its naïve and ill-informed reading of Afghan politics until after bin Laden bombed the U.S. embassies in Nairobi and Dar es Salaam on August 7, 1998.

FAIR-WEATHER FRIENDS

A cooperative agreement between the United States and Pakistan was anything but natural or based on mutual interests. Only two weeks after radical students seized the American embassy in Tehran on November 5, 1979, a similar group of Islamic radicals burned to the ground the American embassy in Islamabad as Zia's troops stood idly by. But the United States was willing to overlook almost anything the Pakistani dictator did in order to keep him committed to the anti-Soviet jihad. After the Soviet invasion, Brzezinski wrote to Carter: "This will require a review of our policy toward Pakistan, more guarantees to it, more arms aid, and, alas, a decision that our security policy toward Pakistan cannot be dictated by our non-proliferation policy." History will record whether Brzezinski made an intelligent decision in giving a green light to Pakistan's development of nuclear weapons in return for assisting the anti-Soviet insurgency.

Pakistan's motives in Afghanistan were very different from those of the United States. Zia was a devout Muslim and a passionate supporter of Islamist groups in his own country, in Afghanistan, and throughout the world. But he was not a fanatic and had some quite practical reasons for supporting Islamic radicals in Afghanistan. He probably would not have been included in the U.S. embassy's annual "beard census" of Pakistani military officers, which recorded the number of officer graduates and serving generals who kept their beards in accordance with Islamic traditions as an unobtrusive measure of increasing or declining religious radicalism; Zia had only a mustache.

From the beginning, Zia demanded that all weapons and aid for the Afghans from whatever source pass through ISI hands. The CIA was delighted to agree. Zia feared above all that Pakistan would be squeezed between a Soviet-dominated Afghanistan and a hostile India. He also had to guard against a Pashtun independence movement that, if successful, would break up Pakistan. In other words, he backed the Islamic militants in Afghanistan and Pakistan on religious grounds but was quite prepared to use them strategically. In doing so, he laid the foundations for Pakistan's anti-Indian insurgency in Kashmir in the 1990s.

Zia died in a mysterious plane crash on August 17, 1988, four months after the signing of the Geneva Accords on April 14, 1988, which ratified the formal terms of the Soviet withdrawal from Afghanistan. As the Soviet troops departed, Hekmatyar embarked on a clandestine plan to eliminate his rivals and establish his

Islamic party, dominated by the Muslim Brotherhood, as the most powerful national force in Afghanistan. The United States scarcely paid attention, but continued to support Pakistan. With the fall of the Berlin Wall in 1989 and the implosion of the USSR in 1991, the United States lost virtually all interest in Afghanistan. Hekmatyar was never as good as the CIA thought he was, and with the creation in 1994 of the Taliban, both Pakistan and Saudi Arabia transferred their secret support. This new group of jihadis proved to be the most militarily effective of the warring groups. On September 26, 1996, the Taliban conquered Kabul. The next day they killed the formerly Soviet-backed ex-president Najibullah, expelled eight thousand female undergraduate students from Kabul University, and fired a similar number of women schoolteachers. As the mujahideen closed in on his palace, Najibullah told reporters: "If fundamentalism comes to Afghanistan, war will continue for many years. Afghanistan will turn into a center of world smuggling for narcotic drugs. Afghanistan will be turned into a center for terrorism." His comments would prove all too accurate.

Pakistan's military intelligence officers hated Benazir Bhutto, Zia's elected successor, but she, like all post-Zia heads of state, including General Pervez Musharraf, supported the Taliban in pursuit of Zia's "dream"—a loyal, Pashtun-led Islamist government in Kabul. Coll explains:

> Every Pakistani general, liberal or religious, believed in the jihadists by 1999, not from personal Islamic conviction, in most cases, but because the jihadists had proved themselves over many years as the one force able to frighten, flummox and bog down the Hindu-dominated Indian army. About a dozen Indian divisions had been tied up in Kashmir during the late 1990s to suppress a few thousand well-trained, paradise-seeking

Islamist guerrillas. What more could Pakistan ask? The jihad-ist guerrillas were a more practical day-to-day strategic defense against Indian hegemony than even a nuclear bomb. To the west, in Afghanistan, the Taliban provided geopolitical "stra-tegic depth" against India and protection from rebellion by Pakistan's own restive Pashtun population. For Musharraf, as for many other liberal Pakistani generals, jihad was not a call-ing, it was a professional imperative. It was something he did at the office. At quitting time he packed up his briefcase, straightened the braid on his uniform, and went home to his normal life.

If the CIA understood any of this, it never let on to its superi-ors in Washington, and Charlie Wilson, a highly paid Pakistani lobbyist and former congressman for East Texas (who "used his trips to the Afghan frontier in part to impress upon a succession of girlfriends how powerful he was"), was anything but forth-coming with Congress about what was really going on. During the 1980s, Wilson had used his power on the House Appropriations Committee to supply all the advanced weapons the CIA might want in Afghanistan. Coll remarks that Wilson "saw the mujahi-deen through the prism of his own whisky-soaked romanticism, as noble savages fighting for freedom, as almost biblical figures."

ENTER BIN LADEN AND THE SAUDIS

Saudi Arabian motives were different from those of both the United States and Pakistan. Saudi Arabia is, after all, the only modern nation-state created by jihad. The Saudi royal family, which came to power at the head of a movement of Wahhabi reli-gious fundamentalists, espoused Islamic radicalism in order to keep it under their control, at least domestically. "Middle-class, pious Saudis flush with oil wealth," Coll writes, "embraced the Afghan cause as American churchgoers might respond to an African famine or a Turkish earthquake":

> The money flowing from the kingdom arrived at the Afghan frontier in all shapes and sizes: gold jewelry dropped on offering plates by merchants' wives in Jedda mosques; bags of cash delivered by businessmen to Riyadh charities as zakat, an annual Islamic tithe; fat checks written from semi-official government accounts by minor Saudi princes; bountiful proceeds raised in annual telethons led by Prince Salman, the governor of Riyadh.

Richest of all were the annual transfers from the Saudi General Intelligence Department, or Istakhbarat, to the CIA's Swiss bank accounts.

From the moment that agency money and weapons started to flow to the mujahideen in late 1979, Saudi Arabia matched the U.S. payments dollar for dollar. They also bypassed the ISI and supplied funds directly to the groups in Afghanistan they favored, including the one led by their own pious young millionaire Osama bin Laden. According to the CIA's Milton Bearden, private Saudi and Arab funding of up to $25 million a month flowed to Afghan Islamist armies. Equally important, Pakistan trained between 16,000 and 18,000 fresh Muslim recruits on the Afghan frontier every year, and another 6,500 or so were instructed by Afghans inside the country beyond ISI control. Most of these eventually joined bin Laden's private army of 35,000 "Arab Afghans."

Much to the confusion of the Americans, moderate Saudi leaders, such as Prince Turki, the intelligence chief, supported the Saudi backing of fundamentalists so long as they were in Afghanistan and not in Saudi Arabia. A graduate of a New Jersey prep school and a member of Bill Clinton's class of 1964 at Georgetown

University, Turki belonged to the pro-Western, modernizing wing of the Saudi royal family. But that did not make him pro-American. Turki saw Saudi Arabia in continual competition with its powerful Shia neighbor Iran. He needed credible Sunni, pro-Saudi Islamist clients to compete with Iran's clients, especially in countries like Pakistan and Afghanistan, which have sizable Shia populations.

Prince Turki was also irritated by the United States' loss of interest in Afghanistan after its Cold War skirmish with the Soviet Union. He understood that the United States would ignore Saudi aid to Islamists so long as his country kept oil prices under control and cooperated with the Pentagon on the building of military bases. Like many Saudi leaders, Turki probably underestimated the longer-term threat of Islamic militancy to the Saudi royal house but, as Coll observes, "Prince Turki and other liberal princes found it easier to appease their domestic Islamist rivals by allowing them to proselytize and make mischief abroad than to confront and resolve these tensions at home." In Riyadh, the CIA made almost no effort to recruit paid agents or collect intelligence. The result was that Saudi Arabia worked continuously to enlarge the ISI's proxy jihad forces in both Afghanistan and Kashmir, and the Saudi Ministry for the Propagation of Virtue and the Prevention of Vice, the kingdom's religious police, tutored and supported the Taliban's own Islamic police force.

By the late 1990s, after the embassy bombings in East Africa, the CIA and the White House awoke to the Islamist threat, but they defined it almost exclusively in terms of Osama bin Laden's leadership of al-Qaeda and failed to see the larger context. They did not target the Taliban, Pakistani military intelligence, or the funds flowing to the Taliban and al-Qaeda from Saudi Arabia and the United Arab Emirates. Instead, they devoted themselves to trying to capture or kill bin Laden. Coll's chapters on the hunt for the al-Qaeda leader are entitled "You Are to Capture Him Alive," "We Are at War," and "Is There Any Policy?" but he might more accurately have called them "Keystone Kops" or "The Gang That Couldn't Shoot Straight."

On February 23, 1998, bin Laden summoned newspaper and TV reporters to the camp at Khost that the CIA had built for him at the height of the anti-Soviet jihad. He announced the creation of a new organization—the International Islamic Front for Jihad against Jews and Crusaders—and issued a manifesto saying that "to kill and fight Americans and their allies, whether civilian or military, is an obligation for every Muslim who is able to do so in any country." On August 7, he and his associates put this manifesto into effect with devastating truck bombings of the U.S. embassies in Kenya and Tanzania.

The CIA had already identified bin Laden's family compound in the open desert near Kandahar Airport, a collection of buildings called Tarnak Farm. It's possible that more satellite footage had by then been taken of this site than of any other place on earth; one famous picture seems to show bin Laden standing outside one of his wives' homes. The agency conceived an elaborate plot to kidnap bin Laden from Tarnak Farm with the help of Afghan operatives and spirit him out of the country, but CIA director George Tenet canceled the project because of the high risk of civilian casualties; he was resented within the agency for his timidity. Meanwhile, the White House stationed submarines in the northern Arabian Sea with the map coordinates of Tarnak Farm preloaded into their missile guidance systems. They were waiting for hard evidence from the CIA that bin Laden was in residence.

Within days of the East Africa bombings, Clinton signed a top secret Memorandum of Notification authorizing the CIA to use lethal force against bin Laden. On August 20, 1998, he ordered seventy-five cruise missiles, costing $750,000 each, to be fired at the

Zawhar Kili camp (about seven miles south of Khost), the site of a major al-Qaeda meeting. The attack killed twenty-one Pakistanis but bin Laden was forewarned, perhaps by Saudi intelligence. Two of the missiles fell short into Pakistan, causing Islamabad to denounce the U.S. action. At the same time, the United States fired thirteen cruise missiles into a chemical plant in Khartoum: the CIA claimed that the plant was partly owned by bin Laden and that it was manufacturing nerve gas. The agency knew none of this was true.

Clinton had publicly confessed to his sexual liaison with Monica Lewinsky on August 17, and many critics around the world conjectured that both attacks were diversionary measures. (The film *Wag the Dog* had just come out, in which a president in the middle of an election campaign is charged with molesting a Girl Scout; the script makes it seem as if he's gone to war against Albania to distract people's attention.) As a result, Clinton became more cautious, and he and his aides began seriously to question the quality of CIA information. The U.S. bombing in May 1999 of the Chinese embassy in Belgrade, allegedly because of faulty intelligence, further discredited the agency. A year later, Tenet fired one intelligence officer and reprimanded six managers, including a senior official, for their bungling of that incident.

The Clinton administration made two more attempts to get bin Laden. During the winter of 1998–99, the CIA confirmed that a large party of Persian Gulf dignitaries had flown into the Afghan desert for a falcon hunting party, and that bin Laden had joined them. The CIA called for an attack on their encampment, until Richard Clarke, Clinton's counterterrorism aide, discovered that among the hosts of the gathering were royalty from the United Arab Emirates. Clarke had been instrumental in a 1998 deal to sell eighty F-16 military jets to the UAE, which was also a crucial supplier of oil and gas to America and its allies. The strike was called off.

THE CIA AS A SECRET PRESIDENTIAL ARMY

Throughout the 1990s, the Clinton administration devoted major resources to the development of a long-distance drone aircraft called Predator, invented by the former chief designer for the Israeli air force, who had immigrated to the United States. In its nose was mounted a Sony digital TV camera, similar to the ones used by news helicopters reporting on freeway traffic or on O. J. Simpson's fevered ride through Los Angeles. By the turn of the century, agency experts had also added a Hellfire antitank missile to the Predator and tested it on a mockup of Tarnak Farm in the Nevada desert. This new weapons system made it possible to kill bin Laden instantly if the camera spotted him. Unfortunately for the CIA, on one of its flights from Uzbekistan over Tarnak Farm the Predator photographed as a target a child's wooden swing. To his credit, Clinton held back on using the Hellfire because of the virtual certainty of killing bystanders, and Tenet, scared of being blamed for another failure, suggested that responsibility for the armed Predator's use be transferred to the Air Force.

When the new Republican administration came into office, it was deeply uninterested in bin Laden and terrorism even though the outgoing national security adviser, Sandy Berger, warned National Security Adviser Condoleezza Rice that it would be George W. Bush's most serious foreign policy problem. On August 6, 2001, the CIA delivered its daily briefing to Bush at his ranch in Crawford, Texas, with the headline "Bin Laden determined to strike in U.S.," but the president seemed not to notice. Slightly more than a month later, Osama bin Laden successfully brought off perhaps the most significant example of asymmetric warfare in the history of international relations.

Coll has written a powerful indictment of the CIA's myopia and incompetence, but he seems to be of two minds. He occasionally indulges in flights of pro-CIA rhetoric, describing it, for example, as a "vast, pulsing, self-perpetuating, highly sensitive network on continuous alert" whose "listening posts were attuned to even the most isolated and dubious evidence of pending attacks" and whose "analysts were continually encouraged to share information as widely as possible among those with appropriate security clearances." This is nonsense: the early-warning functions of the CIA were upstaged decades ago by covert operations.

Coll acknowledges that every president since Truman, once he discovered that he had a totally secret, financially unaccountable private army at his personal disposal, found its deployment irresistible. But covert operations usually became entangled in hopeless webs of secrecy and invariably led to more blowback. Richard Clarke argues that "the CIA used its classification rules not only to protect its agents but also to deflect outside scrutiny of its covert operations," and Peter Tomsen, the former U.S. ambassador to the Afghan resistance during the late 1980s, concludes that "America's failed policies in Afghanistan flowed in part from the compartmented, top secret isolation in which the CIA always sought to work." Excessive bureaucratic secrecy lies at the heart of the agency's failures.

Given the agency's clear role in causing the disaster of September 11, 2001, what we need today is not a new intelligence czar but an end to the secrecy behind which the CIA hides and avoids accountability for its actions. To this day, the CIA continues grossly to distort any and all attempts at a constitutional foreign policy. Although Coll doesn't go on to draw the conclusion, I believe the CIA has outlived any Cold War justification it once might have had and should simply be abolished.

2

EMPIRE v. DEMOCRACY

January 30, 2007

History tells us that one of the most unstable political combinations is a country—like the United States today—that tries to be a domestic democracy *and* a foreign imperialist. Why this is so can be a very abstract subject. Perhaps the best way to offer my thoughts on this is to say a few words about my book *Nemesis* and explain why I gave it the subtitle *The Last Days of the American Republic*. *Nemesis* is the third book to have grown out of my research over the past eight years. I never set out to write a trilogy on our increasingly endangered democracy, but as I kept stumbling on ever more evidence of the legacy of the imperialist pressures we put on many other countries as well as the nature and size of our military empire, one book led to another.

Professionally, I am a specialist in the history and politics of East Asia. In 2000, I published *Blowback: The Costs and Consequences of American Empire*, because my research on China, Japan, and the two Koreas persuaded me that our policies there would have serious future consequences. The book was noticed at the time, but only after 9/11 did the CIA term I adapted for the title—"blowback"—become a household word and my volume a best seller.

I had set out to explain how exactly our government came to be so hated around the world. As a CIA term of tradecraft, "blowback" does not just mean retaliation for things our government has done to, and in, foreign countries. It refers specifically to retaliation for illegal operations carried out abroad *that were kept totally secret from the American public.* These operations have included the clandestine overthrow of governments various administrations did not like, the training of foreign militaries in the techniques of state terrorism, the rigging of elections in foreign countries, and interference with the economic viability of countries that seemed to threaten the interests of influential American corporations, as well as the torture or assassination of selected foreigners. The fact that these actions were, at least originally, secret means that when retaliation does come—as it did so spectacularly on September 11, 2001—the American public is incapable of putting the events in context. Not surprisingly, then, Americans tend to support speedy acts of revenge intended to punish the actual, or alleged, perpetrators. These moments of lashing out, of course, only prepare the ground for yet another cycle of blowback.

A WORLD OF BASES

As a continuation of my own analytical odyssey, I then began doing research on the network of 737 American military bases we maintained around the world (according to the Pentagon's own 2005 official inventory). Not including the Iraq and Afghanistan conflicts, we now station more than half a million U.S. troops, spies, contractors, dependents, and others on military bases located in more than 130 countries, many of them presided over by dictatorial regimes that have given their citizens no say in the decision to let us in.

As but one striking example of imperial basing policy: For the past sixty-one years, the U.S. military has garrisoned the small Japanese island of Okinawa with 37 bases. Smaller than Kauai in the Hawaiian Islands, Okinawa is home to 1.3 million people who live cheek by jowl with 17,000 Marines of the 3rd Marine Division and the largest U.S. installation in East Asia, Kadena Air Force Base. There have been many Okinawan protests against the rapes, crimes, accidents, and pollution caused by this sort of concentration of American troops and weaponry, but so far the U.S. military—in collusion with the Japanese government—has ignored them. My research into our base world resulted in *The Sorrows of Empire: Militarism, Secrecy, and the End of the Republic*, written during the run-up to the Iraq invasion.

As our occupations of Afghanistan and Iraq turned into major fiascoes, discrediting our military leadership, ruining our public finances, and bringing death and destruction to hundreds of thousands of civilians in those countries, I continued to ponder the issue of empire. In these years, it became ever clearer that George W. Bush, Dick Cheney, and their supporters were claiming, and actively assuming, powers specifically denied to a president by our Constitution. It became no less clear that Congress had almost completely abdicated its responsibilities to balance the power of the executive branch. It remains to be seen whether these tendencies can, in the long run, be controlled, let alone reversed.

Until the 2004 presidential election, ordinary citizens of the United States could at least claim that our foreign policy, including our illegal invasion of Iraq, was the work of George Bush's administration and that we had not put him in office. After all, in 2000, Bush lost the popular vote and was appointed president thanks to the intervention of the Supreme Court in a 5–4 decision. But in November 2004, regardless of claims about voter fraud, Bush actually won the popular vote by over 3.5 million ballots, making his regime and his wars ours.

Whether Americans intended it or not, we came to be seen around the world as approving the torture of captives at Abu Ghraib prison in Iraq, at Bagram Air Base in Kabul, at Guantánamo Bay, Cuba, and at a global network of secret CIA prisons, as well as having endorsed Bush's claim that as commander in chief in "wartime" he was beyond all constraints of the Constitution or international law. We were saddled with a rigged economy based on record-setting trade and fiscal deficits, the most secretive and intrusive government in our country's memory, and the pursuit of "preventive" war as a basis for foreign policy. Don't forget as well the potential epidemic of nuclear proliferation as other nations attempted to adjust to and defend themselves against Bush's preventive wars, while our own already staggering nuclear arsenal expanded toward first-strike primacy and we expended unimaginable billions on futuristic ideas for warfare in outer space.

THE CHOICE AHEAD

By the time I came to write *Nemesis*, I no longer doubted that maintaining our empire abroad required resources and commitments that would inevitably undercut, or simply skirt, what was left of our domestic democracy and that might, in the end, produce a military dictatorship or—far more likely—its civilian equivalent. The combination of huge standing armies, almost continuous wars, an ever growing economic dependence on the military-industrial complex and the making of weaponry, and ruinous military expenses as well as a vast, bloated "defense" budget, not to speak of the creation of a whole second Defense Department (known as the Department of Homeland Security), has been destroying our republican structure of governing in favor of an imperial presidency. By "republican" structure I mean of course the separation of powers and the elaborate checks and balances that the founders of our country wrote into the Constitution as the main bulwarks against dictatorship and tyranny, which they greatly feared.

We are on the brink of losing our democracy for the sake of keeping our empire. Once a nation starts down that path, the dynamics that apply to all empires come into play—isolation, overstretch, the uniting of local and global forces opposed to imperialism, and in the end bankruptcy.

History is instructive on this dilemma. If we choose to keep our empire, as the Roman republic did, we will certainly lose our democracy and grimly await the eventual blowback that imperialism generates. There is an alternative, however. We could, like the British Empire after World War II, keep our democracy by giving up our empire. The British did not do a particularly brilliant job of liquidating their empire, and there were several clear cases in which British imperialists defied their nation's commitment to democracy in order to hang on to foreign privileges. The war against the Kikuyu in Kenya in the 1950s and the Anglo-French-Israeli invasion of Egypt in 1956 are particularly savage examples of that. But the overall thrust of postwar British history is clear: the people of the British Isles chose democracy over imperialism.

In her book *The Origins of Totalitarianism*, the political philosopher Hannah Arendt offered the following summary of British imperialism and its fate:

> On the whole it was a failure because of the dichotomy between the nation-state's legal principles and the methods needed to

oppress other people permanently. This failure was neither necessary nor due to ignorance or incompetence. British imperialists knew very well that "administrative massacres" could keep India in bondage, but they also knew that public opinion at home would not stand for such measures. Imperialism could have been a success if the nation-state had been willing to pay the price, to commit suicide and transform itself into a tyranny. It is one of the glories of Europe, and especially of Great Britain, that she preferred to liquidate the empire.

I agree with this judgment. When one looks at Prime Minister Tony Blair's unnecessary and futile support of Bush's invasion and occupation of Iraq, one can only conclude that it was an atavistic response, that it represented a British longing to relive the glories—and cruelties—of a past that should have been ancient history.

As a form of government, imperialism does not seek or require the consent of the governed. It is a pure form of tyranny. The American attempt to combine domestic democracy with such tyrannical control over foreigners is hopelessly contradictory and hypocritical. A country can be democratic or it can be imperialistic, but it cannot be both.

THE ROAD TO IMPERIAL BANKRUPTCY

The American political system failed to prevent this combination from developing—and may now be incapable of correcting it. The evidence strongly suggests that the legislative and judicial branches of our government have become so servile in the presence of the imperial presidency that they have largely lost the ability to respond in a principled and independent manner. Even when Congress stirs, there seems to be a deep sense of helplessness.

Various members of Congress have already attempted to explain how the one clear power they retain—to cut off funds for a disastrous program—is not one they are currently prepared to use.

So the question becomes, if not Congress, could the people themselves restore constitutional government? A grassroots movement to abolish secret government, to bring the CIA and other illegal spying operations and private armies out of the closet of imperial power and into the light, to break the hold of the military-industrial complex, and to establish genuine public financing of elections may be at least theoretically conceivable. But given the conglomerate control of our mass media and the difficulties of mobilizing our large and diverse population, such an opting for popular democracy, as we remember it from our past, seems unlikely.

It is possible that at some future moment, the U.S. military could actually take over the government and declare a dictatorship (though its commanders would undoubtedly find a gentler, more user-friendly name for it). That is, after all, how the Roman republic ended—by being turned over to a populist general, Julius Caesar, who had just been declared dictator for life. After his assassination and a short interregnum, it was his grandnephew Octavian who succeeded him and became the first Roman emperor, Augustus Caesar. The American military is unlikely to go that route. But one cannot ignore the fact that professional military officers seem to have played a considerable role in getting rid of their civilian overlord, Secretary of Defense Donald Rumsfeld. The new directors of the CIA, its main internal branches, the National Security Agency, and many other key organs of the "defense establishment" are now military (or ex-military) officers, strongly suggesting that the military does not need to take over the government in order to control it. Meanwhile, the all-volunteer army has emerged as an ever more separate institution in our society, its profile less and less like that of the general populace.

Nonetheless, military coups, however decorous, are not part of the American tradition, nor that of the officer corps, which might well worry about how the citizenry would react to a move toward open military dictatorship. Moreover, prosecutions of low-level military torturers from Abu Ghraib prison and killers of civilians in Iraq have demonstrated to enlisted troops that obedience to illegal orders can result in dire punishment in a situation where those of higher rank go free. No one knows whether ordinary soldiers, even from what is no longer in any normal sense a citizen army, would obey clearly illegal orders to oust an elected government or whether the officer corps would ever have sufficient confidence to issue such orders. In addition, the present system already offers the military high command so much—in funds, prestige, and future employment via the famed "revolving door" of the military-industrial complex—that a perilous transition to anything like direct military rule would make little sense under reasonably normal conditions.

Whatever future developments may prove to be, my best guess is that the United States will continue to maintain a façade of constitutional government and drift along until financial bankruptcy overtakes it. Of course, bankruptcy will not mean the literal end of the United States any more than it did for Germany in 1923, China in 1948, or Argentina in 2001–2002. It might, in fact, open the way for an unexpected restoration of the American system—or for military rule, revolution, or simply some new development we cannot yet imagine.

Certainly, such a bankruptcy would mean a drastic lowering of our standard of living, a further loss of control over international affairs, a sudden need to adjust to the rise of other powers, including China and India, and a further discrediting of the notion that the United States is somehow exceptional compared to other nations. We will have to learn what it means to be a far poorer country—and the attitudes and manners that go with it. As Anatol Lieven, author of *America Right or Wrong: An Anatomy of American Nationalism*, observes,

> U.S. global power, as presently conceived by the overwhelming majority of the U.S. establishment, is unsustainable. . . . The empire can no longer raise enough taxes or soldiers, it is increasingly indebted, and key vassal states are no longer reliable. . . . The result is that the empire can no longer pay for enough of the professional troops it needs to fulfill its self-assumed imperial tasks.

In February 2006, the Bush administration submitted to Congress a $439 billion defense appropriation budget for fiscal year 2007. As the country entered 2007, the administration was preparing to present a nearly $100 billion supplementary request to Congress just for the Iraq and Afghan wars. At the same time, the deficit in the country's current account—the imbalance in the trading of goods and services as well as the shortfall in all other cross-border payments from interest income and rents to dividends and profits on direct investments—underwent its fastest ever quarterly deterioration. For 2005, the current account deficit was $805 billion, 6.4 percent of national income. In 2005, the U.S. trade deficit, the largest component of the current account deficit, soared to an all-time high of $725.8 billion, the fourth consecutive year that America's trade debts set records. The trade deficit with China alone rose to $201.6 billion, the highest imbalance ever recorded with any country. Meanwhile, since mid-2000, the country has lost nearly three million manufacturing jobs.

To try to cope with these imbalances, on March 16, 2006, Congress raised the national debt limit from $8.2 trillion to $8.96 trillion. This was the fourth time since George W. Bush took office that it had to be raised. The national debt is the total amount owed by the government and should not be confused with the federal budget deficit, the annual amount by which federal spending exceeds revenue. Had Congress not raised the debt limit, the U.S. government would not have been able to borrow more money and would have had to default on its massive debts.

Among the creditors that finance these unprecedented sums, the two largest are the central banks of China (with $853.7 billion in reserves) and Japan (with $831.58 billion in reserves), both of which are the managers of the huge trade surpluses these countries enjoy with the United States. This helps explain why our debt burden has not yet triggered what standard economic theory would dictate: a steep decline in the value of the U.S. dollar followed by a severe contraction of the American economy when we found we could no longer afford the foreign goods we like so much. So far, both the Chinese and Japanese governments continue to be willing to be paid in dollars in order to sustain American purchases of their exports.

For the sake of their own domestic employment, both countries lend huge amounts to the American treasury, but there is no guarantee of how long they will want, or be able, to do so. Marshall Auerback, an international financial strategist, says we have become a "Blanche DuBois economy" (so named after the leading character in the Tennessee Williams play *A Streetcar Named Desire*) heavily dependent on "the kindness of strangers." Unfortunately, in our case, as in Blanche's, there are ever fewer strangers willing to support our illusions.

So my own hope is that—if the American people do not find a way to choose democracy over empire—at least our imperial venture will end not with a nuclear bang but a financial whimper. From the present vantage point, it certainly seems a daunting challenge for any president (or Congress) from either party even to begin the task of dismantling the military-industrial complex, ending the pall of "national security" secrecy and the "black budgets" that make public oversight of what our government does impossible, and bringing the president's secret army, the CIA, under democratic control. It's evident that Nemesis—in Greek mythology the goddess of vengeance, the punisher of hubris and arrogance—is already a visitor in our country, simply biding her time before she makes her presence known.

3

THE SMASH OF CIVILIZATIONS

July 7, 2005

In the months before he ordered the invasion of Iraq, George Bush and his senior officials spoke of preserving Iraq's "patrimony" for the Iraqi people. At a time when talking about Iraqi oil was taboo, what he meant by patrimony was exactly that—Iraqi oil. In their "joint statement on Iraq's future" of April 8, 2003, George Bush and Tony Blair declared, "We reaffirm our commitment to protect Iraq's natural resources, as the patrimony of the people of Iraq, which should be used only for their benefit." In this they were true to their word. Among the few places American soldiers actually did guard during and in the wake of their invasion were oil fields and the Oil Ministry in Baghdad. But the real Iraqi patrimony, that invaluable human inheritance of thousands of years, was another matter. At a time when American pundits were warning of a future "clash of civilizations," our occupation forces were letting perhaps the greatest of all human patrimonies be looted and smashed.

There have been many dispiriting sights on TV since George Bush launched his ill-starred war on Iraq—the pictures from

Abu Ghraib, Fallujah laid waste, American soldiers kicking down the doors of private homes and pointing assault rifles at women and children. But few have reverberated historically like the looting of Baghdad's museum—or been forgotten more quickly in this country.

TEACHING THE IRAQIS
ABOUT THE UNTIDINESS OF HISTORY

In archaeological circles, Iraq is known as "the cradle of civilization," with a record of culture going back more than seven thousand years. William R. Polk, the founder of the Center for Middle Eastern Studies at the University of Chicago, says, "It was there, in what the Greeks called Mesopotamia, that life as we know it today began: there people first began to speculate on philosophy and religion, developed concepts of international trade, made ideas of beauty into tangible forms, and above all developed the skill of writing." No other places in the Bible except Israel have more history and prophecy associated with them than Babylonia, Shinar (Sumer), and Mesopotamia—different names for the territory that the British around the time of World War I began to call "Iraq," using the old Arab term for the lands of the former Turkish enclave of Mesopotamia (in Greek, "between the [Tigris and Euphrates] rivers"). Most of the early books of Genesis are set in Iraq (see, for instance, Genesis 10:10 and 11:31, Daniel 1–4, and II Kings 24).

The best known of the civilizations that make up Iraq's cultural heritage are the Sumerians, Akkadians, Babylonians, Assyrians, Chaldeans, Persians, Greeks, Romans, Parthians, Sassanids, and Muslims. On April 10, 2003, in a television address, President Bush acknowledged that the Iraqi people are "the heirs of a great civilization that contributes to all humanity." Only two days later, under the complacent eyes of the U.S. Army, the Iraqis would begin to lose that heritage in a swirl of looting and burning.

In September 2004, in one of the few self-critical reports to come out of Donald Rumsfeld's Department of Defense, the Defense Science Board Task Force on Strategic Communication wrote: "The larger goals of U.S. strategy depend on separating the vast majority of non-violent Muslims from the radical-militant Islamist-Jihadists. But American efforts have not only failed in this respect: they may also have achieved the opposite of what they intended." Nowhere was this failure more apparent than in the indifference—even the glee—shown by Rumsfeld and his generals toward the looting on April 11 and 12, 2003, of the National Museum in Baghdad and the burning on April 14, 2003, of the National Library and Archives as well as the Library of Korans at the Ministry of Religious Endowments. These events were, according to Paul Zimansky, a Boston University archaeologist, "the greatest cultural disaster of the last five hundred years." Eleanor Robson of All Souls College, Oxford, said, "You'd have to go back centuries, to the Mongol invasion of Baghdad in 1258, to find looting on this scale." Yet Secretary of Defense Donald Rumsfeld compared the looting to the aftermath of a soccer game and shrugged it off with the comment, "Freedom's untidy.... Free people are free to make mistakes and commit crimes."

The Baghdad archaeological museum has long been regarded as perhaps the richest of all such institutions in the Middle East. It is difficult to say with precision what was lost there in those catastrophic April days in 2003 because up-to-date inventories of its holdings, many never even described in archaeological journals, were also destroyed by the looters or were incomplete thanks to conditions in Baghdad after the Gulf War of 1991. One of the best records, however partial, of its holdings is the catalog of items the museum lent in 1988 to an exhibition held in Japan's ancient capital of Nara entitled Silk Road Civilizations. But, as one museum official said to John Burns of the *New York Times* after the looting, "All gone, all gone. All gone in two days."

A single beautifully illustrated, indispensable book edited by Milbry Polk and Angela M. H. Schuster, *The Looting of the Iraq Museum, Baghdad: The Lost Legacy of Ancient Mesopotamia*, represents the heartbreaking attempt of more than a dozen archaeological specialists on ancient Iraq to specify what was in the museum before the catastrophe, where those objects had been excavated, and the condition of those few thousand items that have been recovered. The editors and authors have dedicated a portion of the royalties from the book to the Iraqi State Board of Antiquities and Heritage.

At a conference on art crimes held in London a year after the disaster, the British Museum's John Curtis reported that at least half of the forty most important stolen objects had not been retrieved and that of some 15,000 items looted from the museum's showcases and storerooms about 8,000 had yet to be traced. Its entire collection of 5,800 cylinder seals and clay tablets, many containing cuneiform writing and other inscriptions some of which go back to the earliest discoveries of writing itself, was stolen. Since then, as a result of an amnesty for looters, about 4,000 of the artifacts have been recovered in Iraq, and over 1,000 have been confiscated in the United States. Curtis noted that random checks of Western soldiers leaving Iraq had led to the discovery of several in illegal possession of ancient objects. Customs agents in the United States then found more. Officials in Jordan have impounded about 2,000 pieces smuggled in from Iraq; in France, 500 pieces; in Italy, 300; in Syria, 300; and in Switzerland, 250. Lesser numbers have been seized in Kuwait, Saudi Arabia, Iran, and Turkey. None of these objects has as yet been sent back to Baghdad.

The 616 pieces that form the famous collection of "Nimrud gold," excavated by the Iraqis in the late 1980s from the tombs of the Assyrian queens at Nimrud, a few miles southeast of Mosul, were saved, but only because the museum had secretly moved them to the subterranean vaults of the Central Bank of Iraq at the time of the first Gulf War. By the time the Americans got around to protecting the bank in 2003, its building was a burnt-out shell filled with twisted metal beams from the collapse of the roof and all nine floors under it. Nonetheless, the underground compartments and their contents survived undamaged. On July 3, 2003, a small portion of the Nimrud holdings was put on display for a few hours, allowing a handful of Iraqi officials to see them for the first time since 1990.

The torching of books and manuscripts in the Library of Korans and the National Library was in itself a historical disaster of the first order. Most of the Ottoman imperial documents and the old royal archives concerning the creation of Iraq were reduced to ashes. According to Humberto Márquez, the Venezuelan writer and author of *Historia Universal de La Destrucción de Los Libros*, about a million books and ten million documents were destroyed by the fires of April 14, 2003. Robert Fisk, the veteran Middle East correspondent of the *Independent* of London, was in Baghdad the day of the fires. He rushed to the offices of the U.S. Marines' Civil Affairs Bureau and gave the officer on duty precise map locations for the two archives and their names in Arabic and English, and pointed out that the smoke could be seen from three miles away. The officer shouted to a colleague, "This guy says some biblical library is on fire," but the Americans did nothing to try to put out the flames.

THE BURGER KING OF UR

Given the black market value of ancient art objects, U.S. military leaders had been warned that the looting of all thirteen national museums throughout the country would be a particularly grave danger in the days after they captured Baghdad and took control of Iraq. In the chaos that followed the Gulf War of 1991, vandals had stolen about four thousand objects from nine different regional museums. In monetary terms, the illegal trade in antiquities is the third most lucrative form of international trade globally, exceeded only by drug smuggling and arms sales. Given the richness of Iraq's past, there are also more than ten thousand significant archaeological sites scattered across the country, only some fifteen hundred of which have been studied. Following the Gulf War, a number of them were illegally excavated and their artifacts sold to unscrupulous international collectors in Western countries and Japan. All this was known to American commanders.

In January 2003, on the eve of the invasion of Iraq, an American delegation of scholars, museum directors, art collectors, and antiquities dealers met with officials at the Pentagon to discuss the forthcoming invasion. They specifically warned that Baghdad's National Museum was the single most important site in the country. McGuire Gibson of the University of Chicago's Oriental Institute said, "I thought I was given assurances that sites and museums would be protected." Gibson went back to the Pentagon twice to discuss the dangers, and he and his colleagues sent several e-mail reminders to military officers in the weeks before the war began. However, a more ominous indicator of things to come was reported in the April 14, 2003, London *Guardian*. Rich American collectors with connections to the White House were busy "persuading the Pentagon to relax legislation that protects Iraq's heritage by prevention of sales abroad." On January 24, 2003, some sixty New York–based collectors and dealers organized themselves into a new group called the American Council for Cultural Policy and met with Bush administration and Pentagon officials to argue that a post-Saddam Iraq should have relaxed antiquities laws.

Opening up private trade in Iraqi artifacts, they suggested, would offer such items better security than they could receive in Iraq.

The main international legal safeguard for historically and humanistically important institutions and sites is the Hague Convention for the Protection of Cultural Property in the Event of Armed Conflict, signed on May 14, 1954. The United States is not a party to that convention, primarily because, during the Cold War, it feared that the treaty might restrict its freedom to engage in nuclear war, but during the 1991 Gulf War the elder Bush's administration accepted the convention's rules and abided by a "no-fire target list" of places where valuable cultural items were known to exist. UNESCO and other guardians of cultural artifacts expected the younger Bush's administration to follow the same procedures in the 2003 war.

Moreover, on March 26, 2003, the Pentagon's Office of Reconstruction and Humanitarian Assistance (ORHA), headed by Lt. Gen. (ret.) Jay Garner—the civil authority the United States had set up for the moment hostilities ceased—sent to all senior U.S. commanders a list of sixteen institutions that "merit securing as soon as possible to prevent further damage, destruction, and/or pilferage of records and assets." The five-page memo dispatched two weeks before the fall of Baghdad also said, "Coalition forces must secure these facilities in order to prevent looting and the resulting irreparable loss of cultural treasures" and that "looters should be arrested/detained." First on Gen. Garner's list of places to protect was the Iraqi Central Bank, which is now a ruin; second was the Museum of Antiquities. Sixteenth was the Oil Ministry, the only place that U.S. forces occupying Baghdad actually defended. Martin Sullivan, chair of the President's Advisory Committee on Cultural Property for the previous eight years, and Gary Vikan, director of the Walters Art Museum in Baltimore and a member of the committee, both resigned to protest the failure of CENTCOM to obey orders. Sullivan said it was "inexcusable" that the museum should not have had the same priority as the Oil Ministry.

As we now know, the American forces made no effort to prevent the looting of the great cultural institutions of Iraq, its soldiers simply watching vandals enter and torch the buildings. Saïd Arjomand, an editor of the journal *Studies on Persianate Societies* and a professor of sociology at the State University of New York at Stony Brook, wrote, "Our troops, who have been proudly guarding the Oil Ministry, where no window is broken, deliberately condoned these horrendous events." American commanders claim that, to the contrary, they were too busy fighting and had too few troops to protect the museum and libraries. However, this seems to be an unlikely explanation. During the battle for Baghdad, the U.S. military was perfectly willing to dispatch some two thousand troops to secure northern Iraq's oilfields, and their record on antiquities did not improve when the fighting subsided. At the six-thousand-year-old Sumerian city of Ur with its massive ziggurat, or stepped temple-tower (built in the period 2112–2095 BC and restored by Nebuchadnezzar II in the sixth century BC), the Marines spray-painted their motto, "Semper Fi" (*semper fidelis*, always faithful) onto its walls. The military then made the monument "off limits" to everyone in order to disguise the desecration that had occurred there, including the looting by U.S. soldiers of clay bricks used in the construction of the ancient buildings.

Until April 2003, the area around Ur, in the environs of Nasiriyah, was remote and sacrosanct. However, the U.S. military chose the land immediately adjacent to the ziggurat to build its huge Tallil Air Base with two runways measuring 12,000 and 9,700 feet and four satellite camps. In the process, military engineers moved more than 9,500 truckloads of dirt in order to build 350,000 square feet of hangars and other facilities for aircraft and Predator unmanned drones. They completely ruined the area, the literal heartland of human civilization, for any further archaeological research or future tourism. On October 24, 2003, according to the Global Security Organization, the Army and Air Force Exchange Service built its own modern ziggurat. It "opened its second Burger King at Tallil. The new facility, co-located with [a] Pizza Hut, provided another Burger King restaurant so that more servicemen and women serving in Iraq could, if only for a moment, forget about the task at hand in the desert and get a whiff of that familiar scent that takes them back home."

The great British archaeologist Sir Max Mallowan (husband of Agatha Christie), who pioneered the excavations at Ur, Nineveh, and Nimrud, quotes some classical advice that the Americans might have been wise to heed: "There was danger in disturbing ancient monuments. . . . It was both wise and historically important to reverence the legacies of ancient times. Ur was a city infested with ghosts of the past and it was prudent to appease them."

The American record elsewhere in Iraq is no better. At Babylon, American and Polish forces built a military depot, despite objections from archaeologists. John Curtis, the British Museum's authority on Iraq's many archaeological sites, reported on a visit in December 2004 that he saw "cracks and gaps where somebody had tried to gouge out the decorated bricks forming the famous dragons of the Ishtar Gate" and a "2,600-year-old brick pavement crushed by military vehicles." Other observers say that the dust stirred up by U.S. helicopters has sandblasted the fragile brick façade of the palace of Nebuchadnezzar II, king of Babylon from 605 to 562 BC. The archaeologist Zainab Bahrani reports, "Between May and August 2004, the wall of the Temple of Nabu and the roof of the Temple of Ninmah, both of the sixth century BC, collapsed as a result of the movement of helicopters. Nearby, heavy machines and vehicles stand parked on the remains of a Greek theater from the era of Alexander of Macedon [Alexander the Great]."

And none of this even begins to deal with the massive, ongoing looting of historical sites across Iraq by freelance grave and antiquities robbers, preparing to stock the living rooms of Western collectors. The unceasing chaos and lack of security brought to Iraq in the wake of our invasion have meant that a future peaceful Iraq may hardly have a patrimony to display. It is no small accomplishment of the Bush administration to have plunged the cradle of the human past into the same sort of chaos and lack of security as the Iraqi present. If amnesia is bliss, then the fate of Iraq's antiquities represents a kind of modern paradise.

President Bush's supporters have talked endlessly about his global war on terrorism as a "clash of civilizations." But the civilization we are in the process of destroying in Iraq is part of our own heritage. It is also part of the world's patrimony. Before our invasion of Afghanistan, we condemned the Taliban for their dynamiting of the monumental third-century-AD Buddhist statues at Bamiyan in March 2001. Those were two gigantic statues of remarkable historical value, and the barbarism involved in their destruction blazed in headlines and horrified commentaries in our country. Today, our own government is guilty of far greater crimes when it comes to the destruction of a whole universe of antiquity, and few here, when they consider Iraqi attitudes toward the American occupation, even take that into consideration. But what we do not care to remember, others may recall all too well.

UPDATE: THE PAST DESTROYED
(FIVE YEARS LATER)

August 24, 2008

On April 11, 12, 13, and 14, 2003, the United States Army and United States Marine Corps disgraced themselves and the country they represent in Baghdad, Iraq's capital city. Having invaded Iraq and accepted the status of a military occupying power, they sat in their tanks and Humvees, watching as unarmed civilians looted the Iraqi National Museum and burned down the Iraqi National Library and Archives as well as the Library of Korans of the Ministry of Religious Endowments. Their behavior was in violation of their orders, international law, and the civilized values of the United States. Far from apologizing for these atrocities or attempting to make amends, the U.S. government has in the past five years added insult to injury.

Donald Rumsfeld, then secretary of defense and the official responsible for the actions of the troops, repeatedly attempted to trivialize what had occurred with inane public statements such as "Democracy is messy" and "Stuff happens."

On December 2, 2004, President Bush awarded the Presidential Medal of Freedom, the nation's highest civilian award, to General Tommy Franks, the overall military commander in Iraq at that time, for his meritorious service to the country. (He gave the same award to L. Paul Bremer III, the highest-ranking civilian official in Iraq, and to George Tenet, director of the Central Intelligence Agency, which had provided false information about Saddam Hussein and Iraq to Congress and the people.)

In the five years since the initial looting and pillaging of the Iraqi capital, thieves have stolen at least 32,000 items from some 12,000 archaeological sites across Iraq with no interference whatsoever from the occupying power. No funds have been appropriated by the American or Iraqi governments to protect the most valuable and vulnerable historical sites on earth, even though experience has shown that just a daily helicopter overflight usually scares off looters. In 2006, the World Monuments Fund took the unprecedented step of putting the entire country of Iraq on its list of the most endangered sites. All of this occurred on

George W. Bush's watch and impugned any moral authority he might have claimed.

The U.S. government seems never to have understood that when it began the occupation of Iraq on March 19, 2003, it became legally responsible for what happened to the country's cultural inheritance. After all, the only legal justification for its presence in Iraq is U.N. Security Council Resolution 1483 of May 22, 2003. Both the United States and the United Kingdom voted for this resolution in which they formally acknowledged their status and obligations as occupying powers in Iraq. Among those obligations, specified in the preamble to the resolution, was: "The need for respect for the archaeological, historical, cultural, and religious heritage of Iraq, and for the continued protection of archaeological, historical, cultural, and religious sites, museums, libraries, and monuments." Every politically sentient observer on earth was aware of the Bush administration's contempt for international law and its routine scofflaw behavior since it came to power, but this clause remains an ironclad obligation that will stand up in an international or a domestic U.S. court. On this issue, the United States is an outlaw, waiting to be brought to justice.

In AD 1258 the Mongols descended on Baghdad and pillaged its magnificent libraries. A well-known adage states that the Tigris River ran black from the ink of the countless texts the Mongols trashed, while the streets ran red with the blood of the city's slaughtered inhabitants. The world has never forgotten that medieval act of barbarism, just as it will never forget what the U.S. military unleashed on the defenseless city in 2003 and in subsequent years. There is simply no excuse for what has happened in Baghdad at the hands of the Americans.

4

PEDDLING DEMOCRACY

May 2, 2006

There is something absurd and inherently false about one country trying to impose its system of government or its economic institutions on another. Such an enterprise amounts to a dictionary definition of imperialism. When what's at issue is "democracy," you have the fallacy of using the end to justify the means (making war on those to be democratized), and in the process the leaders of the missionary country are invariably infected with the sins of hubris, racism, and arrogance.

We Americans have long been guilty of these crimes. On the eve of our entry into World War I, William Jennings Bryan, President Woodrow Wilson's first secretary of state, described the United States as "the supreme moral factor in the world's progress and the accepted arbiter of the world's disputes." If there is one historical generalization that the passage of time has validated, it is that the world could not help being better off if the American president had not believed such nonsense and if the United States had minded its own business in the war between the British and German empires. We might well have avoided Nazism, the Bolshevik Revolution, and another thirty to forty years of the exploitation of India, Indonesia, Indochina, Algeria, Korea, the Philippines, Malaya, and virtually all of Africa by European, American, and Japanese imperialists.

We Americans have never outgrown the narcissistic notion that the rest of the world wants (or should want) to emulate us. In Iraq, bringing democracy became the default excuse for our warmongers—it would be perfectly plausible to call them "crusaders" if Osama bin Laden had not already appropriated the term—once the Bush lies about Iraq's alleged nuclear, chemical, and biological threats and its support for al-Qaeda melted away. Bush and his neocon supporters prattled on endlessly about how "the world is hearing the voice of freedom from the center of the Middle East," but the reality was much closer to what Noam Chomsky dubbed "deterring democracy" in a notable 1992 book of that name. We have done everything in our power to see that the Iraqis did not get a "free and fair election," one in which the Shia majority could come to power and ally Iraq with Iran. As Noah Feldman, the Coalition Provisional Authority's law adviser, put it in November 2003, "If you move too fast the wrong people could get elected."

In the election of January 30, 2005, the U.S. military tried to engineer the outcome it wanted ("Operation Founding Fathers"), but the Shiites won anyway. Nearly a year later in the December 15, 2005, elections for the national assembly, the Shiites won again, but Sunni, Kurdish, and American pressure delayed the formation of a government. After a compromise candidate for prime minister was finally selected, two of the most ominous *condottiere* of the Bush administration, Secretary of State Condoleezza Rice and Secretary of Defense Donald Rumsfeld, flew into Baghdad to tell him what he had to do for "democracy"—leaving the unmistakable impression that the new prime minister was a puppet of the United States.

HOLD THE ECONOMIC ADVICE

After Latin America, East Asia is the area of the world longest under America's imperialist tutelage. If you want to know something about the U.S. record in exporting its economic and political institutions, it's a good place to look. But first, some definitions.

The political philosopher Hannah Arendt once argued that democracy was such an abused concept we should dismiss as a charlatan anyone who used the word in serious discourse without first clarifying what he or she meant by it. Therefore, let me indicate what I mean by "democracy."

First, there must be acceptance within a society of the principle that public opinion matters. If it doesn't, as for example in Stalin's Russia, or present-day Saudi Arabia, or the Japanese prefecture of Okinawa under American military domination, then it hardly matters what rituals of American democracy, such as elections, may be practiced.

Second, there must be some internal balance of power or separation of powers, so that it is impossible for an individual leader to become a dictator. If power is concentrated in a single position and its occupant claims to be beyond legal restraints, as has been true in the United States in the Bush years, then democracy becomes attenuated or only pro forma. In particular, I look for the existence and practice of administrative law—in other words, an independent constitutional court with powers to declare null and void laws that contravene democratic safeguards.

Third, there must be some agreed-upon procedure for getting rid of unsatisfactory leaders. Periodic elections, parliamentary votes of no confidence, term limits, and impeachment are various well-known ways to do this, but the emphasis should be on shared institutions.

With that in mind, let's consider the export of the American economic, and then democratic, "model" to Asia. The countries stretching from Japan to Indonesia, with the exception of the former American colony of the Philippines, make up one of the richest regions on earth today. They include the second most productive country in the world, Japan, with a per capita income well in excess of that of the United States, as well as the world's fastest-growing large economy, China's, which has been expanding at a rate of over 9.5 percent per annum for the past two decades. These countries achieved their economic well-being by ignoring virtually every article of wisdom preached in American economics departments and business schools or propounded by various American administrations.

Japan established the regional model for East Asia. In no case did the other high-growth Asian economies follow Japan's path precisely, but they have all been inspired by the overarching characteristic of the Japanese economic system—namely, the combining of the private ownership of property as a genuine right, defensible in law and inheritable, with state control of economic goals, markets, and outcomes. I am referring to what the Japanese call "industrial policy" (*sangyo seisaku*). In American economic theory (if not in practice), industrial policy is anathema. It contradicts the idea of an unconstrained market guided by laissez-faire. Nonetheless, the American military-industrial complex and our elaborate system of "military Keynesianism" rely on a Pentagon-run industrial policy—even as American theory denies that either the military-industrial complex or economic dependence on arms manufacturing is a significant factor in our economic life. We continue to underestimate the high-growth economies of East Asia because of the power of our ideological blinders.

One particular form of American economic influence did greatly affect East Asian economic practice: namely, protectionism and the control of competition through high tariffs and other forms of state discrimination against foreign imports. This was the primary economic policy of the United States from its founding until 1940. Without it, American economic wealth of the sort to which we have become accustomed would have been inconceivable. The East Asian countries have emulated the United States in this respect. They are interested in what the United States does, not what it preaches. That is one of the ways they all got rich. China is today pursuing a variant of the basic Japanese development strategy, even though it does not, of course, acknowledge this.

MARKETING DEMOCRACY

The gap between preaching and self-deception in the way we promote democracy abroad is even greater than in selling our economic ideology. Our record is one of continuous (sometimes unintended) failure, although most establishment pundits try to camouflage this fact.

The Federation of American Scientists has compiled a list of more than two hundred overseas military operations from the end of World War II until September 11, 2001, in which we were involved and typically struck the first blow. The current wars in Afghanistan and Iraq are not included. In no instance did democratic governments come about as a direct result of any of these military activities.

The United States holds the unenviable record of having helped install and then supported such dictators as the shah of

Iran, General Suharto in Indonesia, Fulgencio Batista in Cuba, Anastasio Somoza in Nicaragua, Augusto Pinochet in Chile, and Mobutu Sese Seko in Congo-Zaire, not to mention a series of American-backed militarists in Vietnam and Cambodia until we were finally expelled from Indochina. In addition, we ran one of the most extensive international terrorist operations in history against Cuba and Nicaragua because their struggles for national independence produced outcomes that we did not like.

On the other hand, democracy did develop in some important cases as a result of opposition to our interference—for example, after the collapse of the CIA-installed Greek colonels in 1974; in both Portugal in 1974 and Spain in 1975 after the end of the U.S.-supported fascist dictatorships; after the overthrow of Ferdinand Marcos in the Philippines in 1986; following the ouster of General Chun Doo Hwan in South Korea in 1987; and following the ending of thirty-eight years of martial law on the island of Taiwan in the same year.

One might well ask, however: What about the case of Japan? President Bush often cited our allegedly successful installation of democracy there after World War II as evidence of our skill in this kind of activity. What this experience proved, he contended, was that we would have little difficulty implanting democracy in Iraq. As it happens, though, General Douglas MacArthur, who headed the American occupation of defeated Japan from 1945 to 1951, was himself essentially a dictator, primarily concerned with blocking genuine democracy from below in favor of handpicked puppets and collaborators from the prewar Japanese establishment.

When a country loses a war as crushingly as Japan did the war in the Pacific, it can expect a domestic revolution against its wartime leaders. In accordance with the terms of the Potsdam Declaration, which Japan accepted in surrendering, the State

Department instructed MacArthur not to stand in the way of a popular revolution, but when it began to materialize he did so anyway. He chose to keep Hirohito, the wartime emperor, on the throne (where he remained until his death in 1989) and helped bring officials from the industrial and militarist classes that ruled wartime Japan back to power. Except for a few months in 1993 and 1994, the conservatives of the Liberal Democratic Party then ruled Japan until 2009. In this way, Japan and China became among the longest-lived single-party regimes on earth, both parties—the nucleus of the Liberal Democratic Party and the Chinese Communist Party—having come to power in the same year.*

Equally important in the Japanese case, General MacArthur's headquarters actually wrote the quite democratic Constitution of 1947 and bestowed it on the Japanese people under circumstances in which they had no alternative but to accept it. In her 1963 book *On Revolution*, Hannah Arendt stresses "the enormous difference in power and authority between a constitution imposed by a government upon a people and the constitution by which a people constitutes its own government." She notes that in post–World War I Europe, virtually every case of an imposed constitution led to dictatorship or to a lack of power, authority, and stability.

Although public opinion certainly matters in Japan, its democratic institutions have never been fully tested. The Japanese public knows that its constitution was bestowed by its conqueror, not generated from below by popular action. Japan's stability depends greatly on the ubiquitous presence of the United States,

---

* In an August 2009 election, the Democratic Party defeated the Liberal Democratic Party in a landslide, marking the first time—a few months in 1993–94 excepted—in the post–World War II era that the latter party would not be in power.

which supplies the national defense, and on the fairly evenly distributed wealth that gives the public a stake in the regime. But the Japanese people, as well as those of the rest of East Asia, remain fearful of Japan's ever again being on its own in the world.

While more benign than the norm, Japan's government is typical of the U.S. record abroad in one major respect. Successive American administrations have consistently favored oligarchies that stand in the way of broad popular aspirations—or movements toward nationalist independence from American control. In Asia, in the post–World War II period, we pursued such antidemocratic policies in South Korea, the Philippines, Thailand, Indochina (Cambodia, Laos, and Vietnam), and Japan. In Japan, in order to prevent the Socialist Party from coming to power through the polls, which seemed likely during the 1950s, we secretly supplied funds to the representatives of the old order in the Liberal Democratic Party. We helped bring wartime minister of munitions Nobusuke Kishi to power as prime minister in 1957; split the Socialist Party by promoting and financing a rival Democratic Socialist Party; and, in 1960, backed the conservatives in a period of vast popular demonstrations against the renewal of the Japanese-American Security Treaty. Rather than developing as an independent democracy, Japan became a docile Cold War satellite of the United States—and one with an extremely inflexible political system at that.

THE KOREAN CASE

In South Korea, the United States resorted to far sterner measures. From the outset, we favored those who had collaborated with Japan, whereas North Korea built its regime on the foundation of former guerrilla fighters against Japanese rule. During the 1950s, we backed the aged exile Syngman Rhee as our puppet dictator. (He had actually been a student of Woodrow Wilson's at Princeton early in the century.) When, in 1960, a student movement overthrew Rhee's corrupt regime and attempted to introduce democracy, we instead supported the seizure of power by General Park Chung Hee.

Educated at the Japanese military academy in Manchuria during the colonial period, Park had been an officer in the Japanese army of occupation until 1945. He ruled Korea from 1961 until October 16, 1979, when the chief of the Korean Central Intelligence Agency shot him to death over dinner. The South Korean public believed that the KCIA chief, known to be "close" to the Americans, had assassinated Park on U.S. orders because he was attempting to develop a nuclear weapons program, which the U.S. opposed. (Does this sound familiar?) After Park's death, Major General Chun Doo Hwan seized power and instituted yet another military dictatorship that lasted until 1987.

In 1980, a year after the Park assassination, Chun smashed a popular movement for democracy that broke out in the southwestern city of Kwangju and among students in the capital, Seoul. Backing Chun's policies, the U.S. ambassador argued that "firm anti-riot measures were necessary." The American military then released to Chun's control Korean troops assigned to the U.N. Command to defend the country against a North Korean attack, and he used them to crush the movement in Kwangju. Thousands of prodemocracy demonstrators were killed. In 1981, Chun Doo Hwan would be the first foreign visitor welcomed to the White House by the newly elected Ronald Reagan.

After more than thirty postwar years, democracy finally began to come to South Korea in 1987 via a popular revolution from below. Chun Doo Hwan made a strategic mistake by winning the right to hold the Olympic Games in Seoul in 1988. In the lead-up to the games, students from the many universities in

Seoul, now openly backed by an increasingly prosperous middle class, began to protest American-backed military rule. Chun would normally have used his army to arrest, imprison, and probably shoot such demonstrators, as he had done in Kwangju seven years earlier, but he was held back by the knowledge that if he did so the International Olympic Committee would move the games to some other country. In order to avoid such a national humiliation, Chun turned over power to his coconspirator of 1979–80, General Roh Tae Woo. In order to allow the Olympics to go ahead, Roh instituted a measure of democratic reform, which led in 1993 to the holding of national elections and the victory of a civilian president, Kim Young Sam.

In December 1995, in one of the clearest signs of South Korea's maturing democracy, the government arrested generals Chun Doo Hwan and Roh Tae Woo and charged them with having shaken down Korean big business for bribes—Chun Doo Hwan allegedly took $1.2 billion and Roh Tae Woo $630 million. President Kim then made a very popular decision, letting them be indicted for their military seizure of power in 1979 and for the Kwangju massacre as well. In August 1996, a South Korean court found both Chun and Roh guilty of sedition. Chun was sentenced to death and Roh to twenty-two and a half years in prison. In April 1997, the Korean Supreme Court upheld slightly less severe sentences, something that would have been simply unimaginable for the pro forma Japanese Supreme Court. In December 1997, after peace activist Kim Dae Jung was elected president, he pardoned them both, despite the fact that Chun had repeatedly tried to have Kim killed.

The United States was always deeply involved in these events. In 1989, when the Korean National Assembly sought to investigate what happened at Kwangju on its own, the U.S. government refused to cooperate and prohibited the former American ambassador to Seoul and the former general in command of U.S. Forces Korea from testifying. The American press avoided reporting on these events (while focusing on the suppression of prodemocracy demonstrators in Beijing in June 1989), and most Americans knew next to nothing about them. This cover-up of the costs of military rule and the suppression of democracy in South Korea, in turn, contributed to a growing South Korean hostility toward the United States.

Unlike American-installed or -supported "democracies" elsewhere, South Korea has developed into a genuine democracy. Public opinion is a vital force in the society. A separation of powers has been institutionalized and is honored. Electoral competition for all political offices is intense, with high levels of participation by voters. These achievements came from below, from the Korean people themselves, who liberated their country from American-backed military dictatorship. Perhaps most important, the Korean National Assembly—the parliament—is a genuine forum for democratic debate. I have visited it often and find the contrast with the scripted and empty procedures encountered in the Japanese Diet or the Chinese National People's Congress striking indeed. Perhaps its only rival in terms of democratic vitality in East Asia is the Taiwanese Legislative Yuan. On some occasions, the Korean National Assembly is rowdy; fistfights are not uncommon. It is, however, a true school of democracy, one that came into being despite the resistance of the United States.

THE DEMOCRACY PEDDLERS

Given this history, why should we be surprised that in Baghdad such figures as former head of the Coalition Provisional Authority L. Paul Bremer III, former ambassador John Negroponte, and Ambassador Zalmay Khalilzad, as well as a continuously changing cohort of American major generals fresh from PowerPoint lectures at the American Enterprise Institute, should have produced chaos and probable civil war? None of them has any qualifications at all for trying to "introduce democracy" or American-style capitalism in a highly nationalistic Muslim nation, and even if they did, they could not escape the onus of having terrorized the country through the use of unrestricted military force.

Bremer is a former assistant and employee of Henry Kissinger and General Alexander Haig. Negroponte was the American ambassador to Honduras from 1981 to 1985, when Honduras had the world's largest CIA station and actively participated in the dirty war to suppress Nicaraguan democracy. Khalilzad, the most prominent official of Afghan ancestry in the Bush administration, was a member of the Project for a New American Century, the neocon pressure group that lobbied for a war of aggression against Iraq. The role of the American military in our war there has been an unmitigated disaster on every front, including the deployment of undisciplined, brutal troops at places like the Abu Ghraib prison. All the United States has achieved is to guarantee that Iraqis will hate us for years to come. The situation in Iraq is worse than it was in Japan or Korea and comparable to our tenure in Vietnam. Perhaps it is worth reconsidering what exactly we are so intent on exporting to the world.

PART II

SPIES, ROGUES, AND
MERCENARIES

5

AGENCY OF ROGUES

July 24, 2007

The American people may not know it, but they have some severe problems with one of their official governmental entities, the Central Intelligence Agency. Because of the almost total secrecy surrounding its activities and the lack of cost accounting on how it spends the money covertly appropriated for it within the defense budget, it is impossible for citizens to know what the CIA's approximately 17,000 employees do with, or for, their share of the yearly $44 to $48 billion or more spent on "intelligence." This inability to account for anything at the CIA is, however, only one problem with the agency, and hardly the most serious one either.

There have been two criminal trials in Italy and Germany against several dozen CIA officials for felonies committed in those countries, including kidnapping people with a legal right to be in Germany and Italy, illegally transporting them to countries such as Egypt and Jordan for torture, and causing them to "disappear" into secret foreign or CIA-run prisons outside the United States without any form of due process of law.*

The possibility that CIA funds were simply being ripped off by insiders was also acute. The CIA's former number three official, its executive director and chief procurement officer, Kyle "Dusty" Foggo, was indicted in San Diego for corruptly funneling contracts for water, air services, and armored vehicles to a lifelong friend and defense contractor, Brent Wilkes, who was unqualified to perform the services being sought. In return, Wilkes treated Foggo to thousands of dollars' worth of vacation trips and dinners, and promised him a top job at his company when he retired from the CIA.**

Thirty years ago, in a futile attempt to provide some check on endemic misbehavior by the CIA, the administration of Gerald Ford created the President's Intelligence Oversight Board. It was to be a civilian watchdog over the agency. A 1981 executive order by President Ronald Reagan made the board permanent and gave it the mission of identifying CIA violations of the law (while keeping them secret in order not to endanger national security). Through five previous administrations, members of the board— all civilians not employed by the government—actively reported on and investigated some of the CIA's most secret operations that seemed to breach legal limits.

However, on July 15, 2007, John Solomon of the *Washington Post* reported that for the first five and a half years of the Bush

---

* In November 2009, an Italian court convicted twenty-two CIA operatives and a U.S. Air Force colonel on kidnapping charges related to the snatching of Hassan Mustafa Osama Nasr, a radical Egyptian imam also known as Abu Omar, off a Milan street in 2003. The Americans were all tried in absentia and each received a five-year prison term, with the exception of former Milan CIA station chief Robert Seldon Lady, who was sentenced to eight years for leading the kidnapping operation.
** After pleading guilty to wire fraud and acknowledging that he had conspired to swindle the government, Foggo was, in February 2009, sentenced to thirty-seven months in prison.

administration, the Intelligence Oversight Board did nothing—no investigations, no reports, no questioning of CIA officials. It evidently found no reason to inquire into the interrogation methods agency operatives employed at secret prisons, or the transfer of captives to countries that use torture, or domestic wiretapping not warranted by a federal court.

Who were the members of this nonoversight board of see-no-evil, hear-no-evil, speak-no-evil monkeys? The board was led by former Bush economic adviser Stephen Friedman. It included Don Evans, a former commerce secretary and friend of the president, former admiral David Jeremiah, and lawyer Arthur B. Culvahouse. The only thing they accomplished was to express their contempt for a legal order by a former president of the United States.

Corrupt and undemocratic practices by the CIA have prevailed since it was created in 1947. However, as citizens, we have now, for the first time, been given a striking range of critical information necessary to understand how this situation came about and why it has been impossible to remedy. We have a long, richly documented history of the CIA from its post–World War II origins to its failure to supply even the most elementary information about Iraq before the 2003 invasion of that country.

DECLASSIFIED CIA RECORDS

Tim Weiner's book *Legacy of Ashes: The History of the CIA* is important for many reasons, but certainly one is that it brings back from the dead the possibility that journalism can actually help citizens perform elementary oversight on our government. Until Weiner's magnificent effort, I would have agreed with Seymour Hersh that in the current crisis of American governance and foreign policy, the failure of the press has been almost complete. Our journalists have generally not even tried to penetrate the layers of secrecy that the executive branch throws up to ward off scrutiny of its often illegal and incompetent activities. This is the first book I've read in a long time that documents its very important assertions in a way that goes well beyond asking readers merely to trust the reporter.

Weiner, a *New York Times* correspondent, has been working on *Legacy of Ashes* for twenty years. He has read more than fifty thousand government documents, mostly from the CIA, the White House, and the State Department. He was instrumental in causing the CIA Records Search Technology (CREST) program of the National Archives to declassify many of them, particularly in 2005 and 2006. He has read more than two thousand oral histories of American intelligence officers, soldiers, and diplomats and has himself conducted more than three hundred on-the-record interviews with current and past CIA officers, including ten former directors of central intelligence. Truly exceptional among authors of books on the CIA, he makes the following claim: "This book is on the record—no anonymous sources, no blind quotations, no hearsay."

Weiner's history contains 154 pages of endnotes keyed to comments in the text. (Numbered notes and standard scholarly citations would have been preferable, as well as an annotated bibliography providing information on where documents could be found, but what he has done is still light-years ahead of competing works.) These notes contain extensive verbatim quotations from documents, interviews, and oral histories. Weiner also observes:

> The CIA has reneged on pledges made by three consecutive directors of central intelligence—[Robert] Gates, [James] Woolsey, and [John] Deutch—to declassify records on nine major covert actions: France and Italy in the 1940s and 1950s;

North Korea in the 1950s; Iran in 1953; Indonesia in 1958; Tibet in the 1950s and 1960s; and the Congo, the Dominican Republic, and Laos in the 1960s.

He is nonetheless able to supply key details on each of these operations from unofficial, but fully identified, sources.

In May 2003, after a lengthy delay, the government finally released the documents on President Dwight D. Eisenhower's engineered regime change in Guatemala in 1954; most of the records from the 1961 Bay of Pigs fiasco in which a CIA-created exile army of Cubans went to their deaths or to prison in a hapless invasion of that island have been released; and the reports on the CIA's 1953 overthrow of Iranian prime minister Muhammad Mossadegh were leaked. Weiner's efforts and his resulting book are monuments to serious historical research in our allegedly "open society." Still, he warns,

> While I was gathering and obtaining declassification authorization for some of the CIA records used in this book at the National Archives, the agency was engaged in a secret effort to reclassify many of those same records, dating back to the 1940s, flouting the law and breaking its word. Nevertheless, the work of historians, archivists, and journalists has created a foundation of documents on which a book can be built.

SURPRISE ATTACKS

As an idea, if not an actual entity, the Central Intelligence Agency came into being as a result of December 7, 1941, when the Japanese attacked the U.S. naval base at Pearl Harbor. It functionally came to an end, as Weiner makes clear, on September 11, 2001, when operatives of al-Qaeda flew hijacked airliners into the

World Trade Center towers in Manhattan and the Pentagon in Washington, D.C. Both assaults were successful surprise attacks.

The Central Intelligence Agency itself was created during the Truman administration in order to prevent future surprise attacks like Pearl Harbor by uncovering planning for them and so forewarning against them. On September 11, 2001, the CIA was revealed to be a failure precisely because it had been unable to discover the al-Qaeda plot and sound the alarm against a surprise attack that would prove almost as devastating as Pearl Harbor. After 9/11, the agency, having largely discredited itself, went into a steep decline and finished the job. Weiner concludes: "Under [CIA director George Tenet's] leadership, the agency produced the worst body of work in its long history: a special national intelligence estimate titled 'Iraq's Continuing Programs for Weapons of Mass Destruction.'" It is axiomatic that as political leaders lose faith in an intelligence agency and quit listening to it, its functional life is over, even if the people working there continue to report to their offices.

In December 1941, there was sufficient intelligence on Japanese activities for the United States to have been much better prepared for a surprise attack. Naval intelligence had cracked Japanese diplomatic and military codes; radar stations and patrol flights had been authorized (but not fully deployed); and strategic knowledge of Japanese past behaviors and capabilities (if not of intentions) was adequate. The FBI had even observed the Japanese consul general in Honolulu burning records in his backyard but reported this information only to Director J. Edgar Hoover, who did not pass it on.

Lacking was a central office to collate, analyze, and put in suitable form for presentation to the president all U.S. government information on an important issue. In 1941, there were plenty of signals about what was coming, but the U.S. government lacked the organization and expertise to distinguish true signals from the background noise of day-to-day communications. In the 1950s, Roberta Wohlstetter, a strategist for the Air Force's think tank the RAND Corporation, wrote a secret study that documented the coordination and communications failings leading up to Pearl Harbor. (Entitled *Pearl Harbor: Warning and Decision*, it was declassified and published by Stanford University Press in 1962.)

THE LEGACY OF THE OSS

The National Security Act of 1947 created the CIA with emphasis on the word "central" in its title. The agency was supposed to become the unifying organization that would distill and write up all available intelligence and offer it to political leaders in a manageable form. The act gave the CIA five functions, four of them dealing with the collection, coordination, and dissemination of intelligence from open sources as well as espionage. It was the fifth function—lodged in a vaguely worded passage that allowed the CIA to "perform such other functions and duties related to intelligence affecting the national security as the National Security Council may from time to time direct"—that turned the CIA into the personal, secret, unaccountable army of the president.

From the very beginning, the agency failed to do what President Truman expected of it, turning at once to cloak-and-dagger projects that were clearly beyond its mandate and only imperfectly integrated into any grand strategy of the U.S. government. Weiner stresses that the true author of the CIA's clandestine functions was George Kennan, the senior State Department authority on the Soviet Union and creator of the idea of "containing" the spread of communism rather than going to war with ("rolling back") the USSR.

Kennan had been alarmed by the ease with which the Soviets were setting up satellites in Eastern Europe and he wanted to "fight fire with fire." Others joined with him to promote this agenda, above all the veterans of the Office of Strategic Services (OSS), a unit that, under General William J. "Wild Bill" Donovan during World War II, had sent saboteurs behind enemy lines, disseminated disinformation and propaganda to mislead Axis forces, and tried to recruit resistance fighters in occupied countries.

On September 20, 1945, Truman had abolished the OSS—a bureaucratic victory for the Pentagon, the State Department, and the FBI, all of which considered the OSS an upstart organization that impinged on their respective jurisdictions. Many of the early leaders of the CIA were OSS veterans and devoted themselves to consolidating and entrenching their new vehicle for influence in Washington. They also passionately believed that they were people with a self-appointed mission of world-shaking importance and that, as a result, they were beyond the normal legal restraints placed on government officials.

From its inception the CIA has labored under two contradictory conceptions of what it was supposed to be doing, and no president has ever succeeded in correcting or resolving this situation. Espionage and intelligence analysis seek to know the world as it is; covert action seeks to change the world, whether it understands it or not. The best CIA exemplar of the intelligence-collecting function was Richard Helms, director of central intelligence (DCI) from 1966 to 1973 (who died in 2002). The great protagonist of cloak-and-dagger work was Frank Wisner, the CIA's director of operations from 1948 until the late 1950s, when he went insane and, in 1965, committed suicide. Wisner never had any patience for espionage and other forms of intelligence collecting.

Weiner quotes William Colby, a future DCI (1973–76), on this subject. The separation of the scholars of the research and analysis division from the spies of the clandestine service created two cultures within the intelligence profession, he said, "separate, unequal, and contemptuous of each other." That critique remained true throughout the CIA's first sixty years.

By 1964, the CIA's clandestine service was consuming close to two-thirds of its budget and 90 percent of the director's time. The agency gathered under one roof Wall Street brokers, Ivy League professors, soldiers of fortune, ad men, newsmen, stunt men, second-story men, and con men. They never learned to work together—the ultimate result being a series of failures in both intelligence and covert operations. In January 1961, on leaving office after two terms, President Eisenhower had already grasped the situation fully. "Nothing has changed since Pearl Harbor," he told his director of central intelligence, Allen Dulles. "I leave a legacy of ashes to my successor." Weiner, of course, draws his title from Eisenhower's metaphor. It would only get worse in the years to come.

The historical record is unequivocal. The United States is hamhanded and brutal in conceiving and executing clandestine operations, and it is simply no good at espionage; its operatives never have enough linguistic and cultural knowledge of target countries to recruit spies effectively. The CIA also appears to be one of the most easily penetrated espionage organizations on the planet. From the beginning, it has repeatedly lost its assets to double agents.

Typically, in the early 1950s, the agency dropped millions of dollars' worth of gold bars, arms, two-way radios, and agents into Poland to support what its top officials believed was a powerful Polish underground movement against the Soviets. In fact, Soviet agents had wiped out the movement years before, turned its key people into double agents, and played the CIA for suckers. As Weiner comments, not only had five years of planning, various agents, and millions of dollars "gone down the drain," but the "unkindest cut might have been [the agency's] discovery that the Poles had sent a chunk of the CIA's money to the Communist Party of Italy."

The story would prove unending. On February 21, 1994, the agency finally discovered and arrested Aldrich Ames, the CIA's chief of counterintelligence for the Soviet Union and Eastern Europe, who had been spying for the USSR for seven years and had sent innumerable U.S. agents before KGB firing squads. Weiner comments, "The Ames case revealed an institutional carelessness that bordered on criminal negligence."

THE SEARCH FOR TECHNOLOGICAL MEANS

Over the years, in order to compensate for these serious inadequacies, the CIA turned increasingly to signals intelligence and other technological means of spying such as U-2 reconnaissance aircraft and satellites. In 1952, the top leaders of the CIA created the National Security Agency—an eavesdropping and cryptological unit—to overcome the agency's abject failure to place any spies in North Korea during the Korean War. The agency debacle at the Bay of Pigs in Cuba led a frustrated Pentagon to create its own Defense Intelligence Agency as a check on the military amateurism of the CIA's clandestine service officers.

Still, technological means, whether satellite spying or electronic eavesdropping, will seldom reveal intentions—and that is the raison d'être of intelligence estimates. As Haviland Smith, who ran operations against the USSR in the 1960s and 1970s, lamented, "The only thing missing is—we don't have anything on Soviet intentions. And I don't know how you get that. And that's *the charter of the clandestine service*" (emphasis in original).

The actual intelligence collected was just as problematic. On the most important annual intelligence estimate throughout the

Cold War—that of the Soviet order of battle—the CIA invariably overstated its size and menace. Then, to add insult to injury, under George H. W. Bush's tenure as DCI (1976–77), the agency tore itself apart over ill-informed right-wing claims that it was actually *underestimating* Soviet military forces. The result was the appointment of "Team B" during the Ford presidency, led by Polish exiles and neoconservative fanatics. It was tasked with "correcting" the work of the Office of National Estimates.

"After the Cold War was over," writes Weiner, "the agency put Team B's findings to the test. Every one of them was wrong." But the problem was not simply one of the CIA succumbing to political pressure. It was also structural: "[F]or thirteen years, from Nixon's era to the dying days of the Cold War, every estimate of Soviet strategic nuclear forces *overstated* [emphasis in original] the rate at which Moscow was modernizing its weaponry."

From 1967 to 1973, I served as an outside consultant to the Office of National Estimates, one of about a dozen specialists brought in to try to overcome the myopia and bureaucratism involved in the writing of these national intelligence estimates. I recall agonized debates over how the mechanical highlighting of worst-case analyses of Soviet weapons was helping to promote the arms race. Some senior intelligence analysts tried to resist the pressures of the Air Force and the military-industrial complex. Nonetheless, the late John Huizenga, an erudite intelligence analyst who headed the Office of National Estimates from 1971 until the wholesale purge of the agency by DCI James Schlesinger in 1973, bluntly said to the CIA's historians:

> In retrospect . . . I really do not believe that an intelligence organization in this government is able to deliver an honest analytical product without facing the risk of political contention. . . . I think that intelligence has had relatively little impact on the

policies that we've made over the years. Relatively none. . . . Ideally, what had been supposed was that . . . serious intelligence analysis could . . . assist the policy side to reexamine premises, render policymaking more sophisticated, closer to the reality of the world. Those were the large ambitions which I think were never realized.

On the clandestine side, the human costs were much higher. The CIA's incessant, almost always misguided attempts to determine how other people should govern themselves; its secret support for fascists (e.g., Greece under George Papadopoulos), militarists (e.g., Chile under Gen. Augusto Pinochet), and murderers (e.g., the Congo under Mobutu Sese Seko); its uncritical support of death squads (El Salvador) and religious fanatics (Muslim fundamentalists in Afghanistan)—all these and more activities combined to pepper the world with blowback movements against the United States.

Nothing has done more to undercut the reputation of the United States than the CIA's "clandestine" (only in terms of the American people) murders of the presidents of South Vietnam and the Congo, its ravishing of the governments of Iran, Indonesia (three times), South Korea (twice), all of the Indochinese states, virtually every government in Latin America, and Lebanon, Afghanistan, and Iraq. The deaths from these armed assaults run into the millions. After 9/11, President Bush asked, "Why do they hate us?" From Iran (1953) to Iraq (2003), the better question would be, "Why would they not?"

THE CASH NEXUS

There is a major exception to this portrait of long-term agency incompetence. "One weapon the CIA used with surpassing skill,"

Weiner writes, "was cold cash. The agency excelled at buying the services of foreign politicians." It started with the Italian elections of April 1948. The CIA did not yet have a secure source of clandestine money and had to raise it secretly from Wall Street operators, rich Italian Americans, and others.

> The millions were delivered to Italian politicians and the priests of Catholic Action, a political arm of the Vatican. Suitcases filled with cash changed hands in the four-star Hassler Hotel. . . . Italy's Christian Democrats won by a comfortable margin and formed a government that excluded communists. A long romance between the [Christian Democratic] party and the agency began. The CIA's practice of purchasing elections and politicians with bags of cash was repeated in Italy—and in many other countries—for the next twenty-five years.

The CIA ultimately spent at least $65 million on Italy's politicians—including "every Christian Democrat who ever won a national election in Italy." As the Marshall Plan to reconstruct Europe got up to speed in the late 1940s, the CIA secretly skimmed the money it needed from Marshall Plan accounts. After the Plan ended, secret funds buried in the annual defense appropriation bill continued to finance the CIA's operations.

After Italy, the CIA moved on to Japan, paying to bring the country's World War II minister of munitions, Nobusuke Kishi, to power as Japan's prime minister (in office from 1957 to 1960). It ultimately used its financial muscle to entrench the (conservative) Liberal Democratic Party in power and turn Japan into a single-party state, which it remained for more than half a century. The cynicism with which the CIA continued to subsidize "democratic" elections in Western Europe, Latin America, and East Asia, starting in the late 1950s, led to disillusionment with the

United States and a distinct blunting of the idealism with which it had waged the early Cold War.

Another major use for its money was a campaign to bankroll alternatives in Western Europe to Soviet-influenced newspapers and books. Attempting to influence the attitudes of students and intellectuals, the CIA sponsored literary magazines in Germany (*Der Monat*) and Britain (*Encounter*), promoted abstract expressionism in art as a radical alternative to the Soviet Union's socialist realism, and secretly funded the publication and distribution of more than two and a half million books and periodicals. Weiner treats these activities rather cursorily. He should have consulted Frances Stonor Saunders's indispensable *The Cultural Cold War: The CIA and the World of Arts and Letters*.

HIDING INCOMPETENCE

Despite all this, the CIA was protected from criticism by its impenetrable secrecy and by the tireless propaganda efforts of such leaders as Allen W. Dulles, director of the agency under President Eisenhower, and Richard Bissell, chief of the clandestine service after Wisner. Even when the CIA seemed to fail at everything it undertook, writes Weiner, "The ability to represent failure as success was becoming a CIA tradition."

After the Chinese intervention in the Korean War, the CIA dropped 212 foreign agents into Manchuria. Within a matter of days, 101 had been killed and the other 111 captured—but this information was effectively suppressed. The CIA's station chief in Seoul, Albert R. Haney, an incompetent army colonel and intelligence fabricator, never suspected that the hundreds of agents he claimed to have working for him all reported to North Korean control officers.

Haney survived his incredible performance in the Korean War because at the end of his tour in November 1952, he helped to arrange for the transportation of a grievously wounded Marine lieutenant back to the United States. That Marine turned out to be the son of Allen Dulles, who repaid his debt of gratitude by putting Haney in charge of the covert operation that—despite a largely bungled, badly directed secret campaign—did succeed in overthrowing the Guatemalan government of President Jacobo Arbenz in 1954. The CIA's handiwork in Guatemala ultimately led to the deaths of 200,000 civilians during the forty years of bloodshed and civil war that followed the sabotage of an elected government for the sake of the United Fruit Company.

Weiner has made innumerable contributions to many hidden issues of postwar foreign policy, some of them still ongoing. For example, during the debate over America's invasion of Iraq after 2003, one of the constant laments was that the CIA did not have access to a single agent inside Saddam Hussein's inner circle. That was not true. Ironically, the intelligence service of France—a country U.S. politicians publicly lambasted for its failure to support us—had cultivated Naji Sabri, Iraq's foreign minister. Sabri told the French agency, and through it the American government, that Saddam Hussein did not have an active nuclear or biological weapons program, but the CIA ignored him. Weiner comments ruefully, "The CIA had almost no ability to analyze accurately what little intelligence it had."

Perhaps the most comical of all CIA clandestine activities—unfortunately all too typical of its covert operations over the last sixty years—was the spying it did in 1994 on the newly appointed American ambassador to Guatemala, Marilyn McAfee, who sought to promote policies of human rights and justice in that country. Loyal to the murderous Guatemalan intelligence service, the CIA had bugged her bedroom and picked up sounds that led their agents to conclude that the ambassador was having a lesbian love affair with her secretary, Carol Murphy. The CIA station chief "recorded her cooing endearments to Murphy." The agency spread the word in Washington that the liberal ambassador was a lesbian without realizing that "Murphy" was also the name of her two-year-old black standard poodle. The bug in her bedroom had recorded her petting her dog. She was actually a married woman from a conservative family.

Back in August 1945, General William Donovan, the head of the OSS, said to President Truman, "Prior to the present war, the United States had no foreign intelligence service. It never has had and does not now have a coordinated intelligence system." Weiner adds, "Tragically, it still does not have one." I agree with Weiner's assessment, but based on his truly exemplary analysis of the Central Intelligence Agency in *Legacy of Ashes*, I do not think that this is a tragedy. Given his evidence, it is hard to believe that the United States would not have been better off if it had left intelligence collection and analysis to the State Department and had assigned infrequent covert actions to the Pentagon.

I believe that this is where we stand today: the CIA has failed badly, and it would be an important step toward a restoration of the checks and balances within our political system simply to abolish it. Some observers argue that this would be an inadequate remedy because what the government now ostentatiously calls "the U.S. Intelligence Community"—complete with its own website—is composed of sixteen discrete and competitive intelligence organizations ready to step into the CIA's shoes. This, however, is a misunderstanding. Most of the members of the so-called intelligence community are bureaucratic appendages of well-established departments or belong to extremely technical units whose functions have nothing at all to do with either espionage or cloak-and-dagger adventures.

The sixteen entities include the intelligence organizations of each military service—the Air Force, Army, Coast Guard, Marine Corps, and Navy—and the Defense Intelligence Agency, which reflect interservice rivalries more than national needs or interests; the departments of Energy, Homeland Security, State, Treasury, and Drug Enforcement Administration, as well as the FBI and the National Security Agency; and the units devoted to satellites and reconnaissance (National Geospatial Intelligence Agency, National Reconnaissance Office). The only one of these units that could conceivably compete with the CIA is the one that I recommend to replace it: the State Department's Bureau of Intelligence and Research (INR). Interestingly enough, it had by far the best record of any U.S. intelligence entity in analyzing Iraq under Saddam Hussein and estimating what was likely to happen if we pursued the Bush administration's misconceived scheme of invading his country. Its work was, of course, largely ignored by the Bush-Cheney White House.

Weiner does not cover every single aspect of the record of the CIA, but his book is one of the best possible places for a serious citizen to begin to understand the depths to which our government has sunk. It also brings home the lesson that an incompetent or unscrupulous intelligence agency can be as great a threat to national security as not having one at all.

6

AN IMPERIALIST COMEDY

January 6, 2008

I have some personal knowledge of congressmen like Charlie Wilson (D–2nd District, Texas, 1973–96) because, for close to twenty years, my representative in the 50th Congressional District of California was Republican Randy "Duke" Cunningham, now serving an eight-and-a-half-year prison sentence for soliciting and receiving bribes from defense contractors. Wilson and Cunningham held exactly the same plummy committee assignments in the House of Representatives—the Defense Appropriations Subcommittee plus the Intelligence Oversight Committee—from which they could dole out large sums of public money with little or no input from their colleagues or constituents.

Both men flagrantly abused their positions—but with radically different consequences. Cunningham went to jail because he was too stupid to know how to game the system by retiring and becoming a lobbyist, whereas Wilson received the Central Intelligence Agency Clandestine Service's first "honored colleague" award ever given to an outsider and went on to become a $360,000 per annum lobbyist for Pakistan.

In a secret ceremony at CIA headquarters on June 9, 1993, James Woolsey, Bill Clinton's first director of central intelligence and one of the agency's least competent chiefs in its checkered history, said: "The defeat and breakup of the Soviet empire is one of the great events of world history. There were many heroes in this battle, but to Charlie Wilson must go a special recognition." One important part of that recognition, studiously avoided by the CIA and most subsequent American writers on the subject, is that Wilson's activities in Afghanistan led directly to a chain of blowback that culminated in the attacks of September 11, 2001, and to the United States' current status as the most widely hated nation on earth.

On May 25, 2003 (the same month in which George W. Bush stood on the flight deck of the USS *Abraham Lincoln* under a White House–prepared "Mission Accomplished" banner and proclaimed "major combat operations" at an end in Iraq), I published a review in the *Los Angeles Times* of the book that provides the data for the film *Charlie Wilson's War*. The original edition of the book carried the subtitle *The Extraordinary Story of the Largest Covert Operation in History—the Arming of the Mujahideen*. The 2007 paperbound edition was subtitled *The Extraordinary Story of How the Wildest Man in Congress and a Rogue CIA Agent Changed the History of Our Times*. Neither the claim that the Afghan operations were covert nor that they changed history is precisely true.

In my review of the book, I wrote,

The Central Intelligence Agency has an almost unblemished record of screwing up every "secret" armed intervention it ever undertook. From the overthrow of the Iranian government in 1953 through the rape of Guatemala in 1954, the Bay of Pigs, the failed attempts to assassinate Fidel Castro of Cuba and

Patrice Lumumba of the Congo, the Phoenix Program in Vietnam, the "secret war" in Laos, aid to the Greek colonels who seized power in 1967, the 1973 killing of President Allende in Chile, and Ronald Reagan's Iran-Contra war against Nicaragua, there is not a single instance in which the agency's activities did not prove acutely embarrassing to the United States and devastating to the people being "liberated." The CIA continues to get away with this bungling primarily because its budget and operations have always been secret and Congress is normally too indifferent to its constitutional functions to rein in a rogue bureaucracy. Therefore the tale of a purported CIA success story should be of some interest.

According to the author of *Charlie Wilson's War*, the exception to CIA incompetence was the arming between 1979 and 1988 of thousands of Afghan mujahideen ("freedom fighters"). The agency flooded Afghanistan with an incredible array of extremely dangerous weapons and "unapologetically mov[ed] to equip and train cadres of high tech holy warriors in the art of waging a war of urban terror against a modern superpower [in this case, the USSR]."

The author of this glowing account, [the late] George Crile, was a veteran producer for the CBS television news show *60 Minutes* and an exuberant Tom Clancy–type enthusiast for the Afghan caper. He argues that the U.S.'s clandestine involvement in Afghanistan was "the largest and most successful CIA operation in history," "the one morally unambiguous crusade of our time," and that "there was nothing so romantic and exciting as this war against the Evil Empire." Crile's sole measure of success is killed Soviet soldiers (about 15,000), which undermined Soviet morale and contributed to the disintegration of the Soviet Union in the period 1989 to 1991. That's the successful part.

However, he never once mentions that the "tens of thousands of fanatical Muslim fundamentalists" the CIA armed are the same people who in 1996 killed nineteen American airmen at Dhahran, Saudi Arabia, bombed our embassies in Kenya and Tanzania in 1998, blew a hole in the side of the USS *Cole* in Aden Harbor in 2000, and on September 11, 2001, flew hijacked airliners into New York's World Trade Center and the Pentagon.

WHERE DID THE "FREEDOM FIGHTERS" GO?

When I wrote those words I did not know (and could not have imagined) that the actor Tom Hanks had already purchased the rights to the book to make into a film in which he would star as Charlie Wilson, with Julia Roberts as his right-wing Texas girlfriend Joanne Herring and Philip Seymour Hoffman as Gust Avrakotos, the thuggish CIA operative who helped pull off this caper.

What to make of the film (which I found rather boring and old-fashioned)? It makes the U.S. government look as if it is populated by a bunch of whoring, drunken sleazebags, so in that sense it's accurate enough. But there are a number of things both the book and the film are suppressing. As I noted in 2003,

> For the CIA legally to carry out a covert action, the president must sign off on—that is, authorize—a document called a "finding." Crile repeatedly says that President Carter signed such a finding ordering the CIA to provide covert backing to the mujahideen *after* the Soviet Union invaded Afghanistan on December 24, 1979. The truth of the matter is that Carter signed the finding on July 3, 1979, *six months before the Soviet invasion*, and he did so on the advice of his national security

adviser, Zbigniew Brzezinski, in order to try to provoke a Russian incursion. Brzezinski has confirmed this sequence of events in an interview with a French newspaper, and former CIA Director [today Secretary of Defense] Robert Gates says so explicitly in his 1996 memoirs. It may surprise Charlie Wilson to learn that his heroic mujahideen were manipulated by Washington like so much cannon fodder in order to give the USSR its own Vietnam. The mujahideen did the job, but as subsequent events have made clear, they may not be all that grateful to the United States.

In the bound galleys of Crile's book, which his publisher sent to reviewers before publication, there was no mention of any qualifications to his portrait of Wilson as a hero and a patriot. Only in an "epilogue" added to the printed book did Crile quote Wilson as saying, "These things happened. They were glorious and they changed the world. And the people who deserved the credit are the ones who made the sacrifice. And then we fucked up the endgame." That's it. Full stop. Director Mike Nichols, too, ends his movie with Wilson's final sentence emblazoned across the screen. And then the credits roll.

Neither a reader of Crile nor a viewer of the film based on his book would know that in talking about the Afghan freedom fighters of the 1980s, we are also talking about the militants of al-Qaeda and the Taliban of the 1990s and 2000s. Amid all the hoopla about Wilson's going out of channels to engineer secret appropriations of millions of dollars to the guerrillas, the reader or viewer would never suspect that when the Soviet Union withdrew from Afghanistan in 1989, President George H. W. Bush promptly lost interest in the place and simply walked away, leaving it to descend into one of the most horrific civil wars of modern times.

Among those supporting the Afghans (in addition to the United States) was the rich, pious Saudi Arabian economist and civil engineer Osama bin Laden, whom we helped by building up his al-Qaeda base at Khost. When bin Laden and his colleagues decided to get even with us for having been used, he had the support of much of the Islamic world. This disaster was brought about by Wilson's and the CIA's incompetence as well as their subversion of all the normal channels of political oversight and democratic accountability within the U.S. government. Charlie Wilson's war thus turned out to have been just another bloody skirmish in the expansion and consolidation of the American empire—and an imperial presidency. The victors were the military-industrial complex and our massive standing armies. The billion dollars' worth of weapons Wilson secretly supplied to the guerrillas ended up being turned on ourselves.

AN IMPERIALIST COMEDY

Which brings us back to the movie and its reception here. (It was banned in Afghanistan.) One of the severe side effects of imperialism in its advanced stages seems to be that it rots the brains of the imperialists. They start believing that they are the bearers of civilization, the bringers of light to "primitives" and "savages" (largely so identified because of their resistance to being "liberated" by us), the carriers of science and modernity to backward peoples, beacons and guides for citizens of the "underdeveloped world."

Such attitudes are normally accompanied by a racist ideology that proclaims the intrinsic superiority and right to rule of "white" Caucasians. Innumerable European colonialists saw the hand of God in Darwin's discovery of evolution, so long as it was understood that He had programmed the outcome of evolution in favor of late-Victorian Englishmen. (For an excellent short book on this subject, check out Sven Lindqvist's *"Exterminate All the Brutes".*)

When imperialist activities produce unmentionable outcomes, such as those well known to anyone paying attention to Afghanistan since about 1990, then ideological thinking kicks in. The horror story is suppressed, or reinterpreted as something benign or ridiculous (a "comedy"), or simply curtailed before the denouement becomes obvious. Thus, for example, Melissa Roddy, a Los Angeles filmmaker with inside information from the *Charlie Wilson* production team, notes that the film's happy ending came about because Tom Hanks, a coproducer as well as the leading actor, "just can't deal with this 9/11 thing."

Similarly, we are told by another insider reviewer, James Rocchi, that the scenario as originally written by Aaron Sorkin of *West Wing* fame included the following line for Avrakotos: "Remember I said this: There's going to be a day when we're gonna look back and say 'I'd give anything if [Afghanistan] were overrun with Godless communists.'" This line is nowhere to be found in the final film.

Today there is ample evidence that when it comes to the freedom of women, education levels, governmental services, relations among different ethnic groups, and quality of life, all were infinitely better under the Afghan communists than under the Taliban *or* the present government of President Hamid Karzai, which evidently controls little beyond the country's capital, Kabul. But Americans don't want to know that—and certainly they get no indication of it from *Charlie Wilson's War,* either the book or the film.

The tendency of imperialism to rot the brains of imperialists was particularly on display in the recent spate of articles and reviews in mainstream American newspapers about the film. For reasons not entirely clear, an overwhelming majority of reviewers concluded that *Charlie Wilson's War* was a "feel-good comedy" (Lou Lumenick in the *New York Post*), a "high-living, hard-partying jihad" (A. O. Scott in the *New York Times*), "a sharp-edged, wickedly funny comedy" (Roger Ebert in the *Chicago Sun-Times*). Stephen Hunter in the *Washington Post* wrote of "Mike Nichols's laff-a-minute chronicle of the congressman's crusade to ram funding through the House Appropriations Committee to supply arms to the Afghan mujahideen," while in a piece entitled "Sex! Drugs! (and Maybe a Little War)," Richard L. Berke in the *New York Times* offered this stamp of approval: "You can make a movie that is relevant and intelligent—and palatable to a mass audience—if its political pills are sugar-coated."

When I saw the film, there was only a guffaw or two from the audience over the raunchy sex and sexism of "good-time Charlie," but certainly no laff-a-minute. The root of this approach to the film probably lies with Tom Hanks himself, who, according to Berke, called it "a serious comedy." A few reviews qualified their endorsement of *Charlie Wilson's War* but still came down on the side of good old American fun. Rick Groen in the Toronto *Globe and Mail*, for instance, thought that it was "best to enjoy *Charlie Wilson's War* as a thoroughly engaging comedy. Just don't think about it too much or you may choke on your popcorn." Peter Rainer noted in the *Christian Science Monitor* that the "comedic *Charlie Wilson's War* has a tragic punch line." These reviewers were thundering along with the herd while still trying to maintain a bit of self-respect.

The handful of truly critical reviews have come mostly from blogs and little-known Hollywood fanzines—with one major exception, Kenneth Turan of the *Los Angeles Times*. In an essay subtitled " 'Charlie Wilson's War' celebrates events that came back to haunt Americans," Turan called the film "an unintentionally sobering narrative of American shouldn't-have" and added that it was "glib rather than witty, one of those films that comes off as being more pleased with itself than it has a right to be."

My own view is that if *Charlie Wilson's War* is a comedy, it's the kind that goes over well with a roomful of louts in a college fraternity house. Simply put, it is imperialist propaganda, and the tragedy is that four and a half years after we invaded Iraq and destroyed it, such dangerously misleading nonsense is still being offered to a gullible public. The most accurate review was James Rocchi's summing-up for *Cinematical*: "*Charlie Wilson's War* isn't just bad history; it feels even more malign, like a conscious attempt to induce amnesia."

7

WARNING:
MERCENARIES AT WORK

July 27, 2008

Most Americans have a rough idea what the term "military-industrial complex" means when they come across it in a newspaper or hear a politician mention it. President Dwight D. Eisenhower introduced the idea to the public in his farewell address of January 17, 1961. "Our military organization today bears little relation to that known by any of my predecessors in peacetime," he said, "or indeed by the fighting men of World War II and Korea. . . . We have been compelled to create a permanent armaments industry of vast proportions. . . . We must not fail to comprehend its grave implications. . . . We must guard against the acquisition of unwarranted influence, whether sought or unsought, by the military-industrial complex."

Although Eisenhower's reference to the military-industrial complex is by now well known, his warning against its "unwarranted influence" has, I believe, largely been ignored. Since 1961, there has been too little serious study, or discussion, of the origins of the military-industrial complex, how it has changed over time, how governmental secrecy has hidden it from oversight by members of Congress or attentive citizens, and how it degrades our constitutional structure of checks and balances.

From its origins in the early 1940s, when President Franklin Delano Roosevelt was building up his "arsenal of democracy," down to the present moment, public opinion has usually assumed that it involved more or less equitable relations—often termed a "partnership"—between the high command and civilian overlords of the United States military and privately owned, for-profit manufacturing and service enterprises. Unfortunately, the truth of the matter is that from the time they first emerged, these relations were never equitable.

In the formative years of the military-industrial complex, the public still deeply distrusted privately owned industrial firms because of the way they had contributed to the Great Depression. Thus, the leading role in the newly emerging relationship was played by the official governmental sector. A deeply popular, charismatic president, FDR sponsored these public-private relationships. They gained further legitimacy because their purpose was to rearm the country, as well as allied nations around the world, against the gathering forces of fascism. The private sector was eager to go along with this largely as a way to regain public trust and disguise its wartime profit making.

In the late 1930s and early 1940s, Roosevelt's use of public-private "partnerships" to build up the munitions industry, and thereby finally overcome the Great Depression, did not go entirely unchallenged. Although he was himself an implacable enemy of fascism, a few people thought that the president nonetheless was coming close to copying some of its key institutions. The leading Italian philosopher of fascism, the neo-Hegelian Giovanni Gentile, once argued that it should more appropriately be called corporatism because it was a merger of state and corporate power.

Some critics were alarmed early on by the growing symbiotic relationship between government and corporate officials because each simultaneously sheltered and empowered the other, while greatly confusing the separation of powers. Since the activities of a corporation are less amenable to public or congressional scrutiny than those of a public institution, public-private collaborative relationships afford the private sector an added measure of security from such scrutiny. These concerns were ultimately swamped by enthusiasm for the war effort and the postwar era of prosperity that the war produced.

Beneath the surface, however, was a less well recognized movement by big business to replace democratic institutions with those representing the interests of capital. This movement is today ascendant. (See Thomas Frank's book *The Wrecking Crew: How Conservatives Rule* for a superb analysis of Ronald Reagan's slogan "Government is not a solution to our problem, government is the problem.") Its objectives have long been to discredit what it called "big government," while capturing for private interests the tremendous sums invested by the public sector in national defense. It may be understood as a slow-burning reaction to what American conservatives believed to be the socialism of the New Deal.

Perhaps the country's leading theorist of democracy, Sheldon S. Wolin, has written in his book *Democracy Incorporated* about what he calls "inverted totalitarianism"—the rise in the United States of totalitarian institutions of conformity and regimentation shorn of the police repression of the earlier German, Italian, and Soviet forms. He warns of "the expansion of private (i.e., mainly corporate) power and the selective abdication of governmental responsibility for the well-being of the citizenry." He also decries the degree to which the so-called privatization of governmental activities has insidiously undercut our democracy, leaving us with the widespread belief that government is no longer needed and that, in any case, it is not capable of performing the functions we have entrusted to it.

Wolin writes:

> The privatization of public services and functions manifests the steady evolution of corporate power into a political form, into an integral, even dominant partner with the state. It marks the transformation of American politics and its political culture, from a system in which democratic practices and values were, if not defining, at least major contributory elements, to one where the remaining democratic elements of the state and its populist programs are being systematically dismantled.

MERCENARIES AT WORK

The military-industrial complex has changed radically since World War II or even the height of the Cold War. The private sector is now fully ascendant. The uniformed air, land, and naval forces of the country as well as its intelligence agencies, including the CIA, the NSA (National Security Agency), the DIA (Defense Intelligence Agency), and even clandestine networks entrusted with the dangerous work of penetrating and spying on terrorist organizations are all dependent on hordes of "private contractors." In the context of governmental national security functions, a better term for these might be "mercenaries" working in private for profit-making companies.

Tim Shorrock, an investigative journalist and the leading authority on this subject, sums up this situation devastatingly in his book *Spies for Hire: The Secret World of Intelligence Outsourcing*. The following quotes are a précis of some of his key findings:

In 2006 . . . the cost of America's spying and surveillance activities outsourced to contractors reached $42 billion, or about 70 percent of the estimated $60 billion the government spends each year on foreign and domestic intelligence. . . . [The] number of contract employees now exceeds [the CIA's] full-time workforce of 17,500. . . . Contractors make up more than half the workforce of the CIA's National Clandestine Service (formerly the Directorate of Operations), which conducts covert operations and recruits spies abroad. . . .

To feed the NSA's insatiable demand for data and information technology, the industrial base of contractors seeking to do business with the agency grew from 144 companies in 2001 to more than 5,400 in 2006. . . . At the National Reconnaissance Office (NRO), the agency in charge of launching and maintaining the nation's photoreconnaissance and eavesdropping satellites, almost the entire workforce is composed of contract employees working for [private] companies. . . . With an estimated $8 billion annual budget, the largest in the IC [intelligence community], contractors control about $7 billion worth of business at the NRO, giving the spy satellite industry the distinction of being the most privatized part of the intelligence community. . . .

If there's one generalization to be made about the NSA's outsourced IT [information technology] programs, it is this: they haven't worked very well, and some have been spectacular failures. . . . In 2006, the NSA was unable to analyze much of the information it was collecting. . . . As a result, more than 90 percent of the information it was gathering was being discarded without being translated into a coherent and understandable format; only about 5 percent was translated from its digital form into text and then routed to the right division for analysis.

The key phrase in the new counterterrorism lexicon is "public-private partnerships." . . . In reality, "partnerships" are a convenient cover for the perpetuation of corporate interests.

Several inferences can be drawn from Shorrock's shocking exposé. One is that if a foreign espionage service wanted to penetrate American military and governmental secrets, its easiest path would not be to gain access to any official U.S. agencies, but simply to get its agents jobs at any of the large intelligence-oriented private companies on which the government has become remarkably dependent. These include Science Applications International Corporation (SAIC), with headquarters in San Diego, California, which typically pays its 42,000 employees higher salaries than if they worked at similar jobs in the government; Booz Allen Hamilton, one of the nation's oldest intelligence and clandestine operations contractors, which, until January 2007, was the employer of Mike McConnell, who then became director of national intelligence and the first private contractor to be named to lead the entire intelligence community; and CACI International, which, under two contracts for "information technology services," ended up supplying some two dozen interrogators to the Army at Iraq's infamous Abu Ghraib prison in 2003. According to Major General Anthony Taguba, who investigated the Abu Ghraib torture and abuse scandal, four of CACI's interrogators were "either directly or indirectly responsible" for torturing prisoners.

Remarkably enough, SAIC has virtually replaced the National Security Agency as the primary collector of signals intelligence for the government. It is the NSA's largest contractor, and that agency is today the company's single largest customer.

There are literally thousands of other profit-making enterprises that work to supply the government with so-called intelligence needs, sometimes even bribing congressmen to fund projects that no one in the executive branch actually wants. This was the case with Congressman Randy "Duke" Cunningham, Republican of California's 50th District, who, in 2006, was sentenced to eight and a half years in federal prison for soliciting bribes from defense contractors. One of the bribers, Brent Wilkes, snagged a $9.7 million contract for his company, ADCS Inc. (Automated Document Conversion Systems), to computerize the century-old records of the Panama Canal dig!

A COUNTRY DROWNING IN EUPHEMISMS

The United States has long had a sorry record when it comes to protecting its intelligence from foreign infiltration, but the situation today seems particularly perilous. One is reminded of the case described in a 1979 book by Robert Lindsey, *The Falcon and the Snowman* (made into a 1985 film of the same name). It tells the true story of two young Southern Californians, one with a high security clearance working for the defense contractor TRW (dubbed "RTX" in the film), and the other a drug addict and minor smuggler. The TRW employee is motivated to act by his discovery of a misrouted CIA document describing plans to overthrow the leftist prime minister of Australia, and the other by a need for money to pay for his addiction.

They decide to get even with the government by selling secrets to the Soviet Union and are exposed by their own bungling. Both are sentenced to prison for espionage. The message of the book (and film) lies in the ease with which they betrayed their country—and how long it took before they were exposed and apprehended. Today, thanks to the staggering overprivatization of the collection and analysis of foreign intelligence, the opportunities for such breaches of security are widespread.

I applaud Shorrock for his extraordinary research into an almost impenetrable subject using only openly available sources. There is, however, one aspect of his analysis with which I differ. This is his contention that the wholesale takeover of official intelligence collection and analysis by private companies is a form of "outsourcing." This term is usually restricted to a business enterprise buying goods and services that it does not want to manufacture or supply in-house. When it is applied to a governmental agency that turns over many, if not all, of its key functions to a risk-averse company trying to make a return on its investment, "outsourcing" simply becomes a euphemism for mercenary activities.

As David Bromwich, a political critic and Yale professor of literature, observed in the *New York Review of Books*:

> The separate bookkeeping and accountability devised for Blackwater, DynCorp, Triple Canopy, and similar outfits was part of a careful displacement of oversight from Congress to . . . [V]ice [P]resident [Cheney] and the stewards of his policies in various departments and agencies. To have much of the work parceled out to private companies who are unaccountable to army rules or military justice, meant, among its other advantages, that the cost of the war could be concealed beyond all detection.

Euphemisms are words intended to deceive. The United States is already close to drowning in them, particularly new words and terms devised, or brought to bear, to justify the American invasion of Iraq—coinages Bromwich highlights such as "regime change," "enhanced interrogation techniques," "the global war on terrorism," "the birth pangs of a new Middle East," a "slight uptick in violence," "bringing torture within the law," "simulated drowning," and, of course, "collateral damage," meaning the slaughter of unarmed civilians by American troops and aircraft followed—rarely—by perfunctory apologies. It is important that the intrusion of unelected corporate officials with hidden profit motives into what are ostensibly public political activities not be confused with private businesses buying Scotch tape, paper clips, or hubcaps.

The wholesale transfer of military and intelligence functions to private, often anonymous operatives took off under Ronald Reagan's presidency and accelerated greatly after 9/11 under George W. Bush and Dick Cheney. Often not well understood, however, is this: the biggest private expansion into intelligence and other areas of government occurred under the presidency of Bill Clinton. He seems not to have had the same antigovernmental and neoconservative motives as the privatizers of both the Reagan and Bush II eras. His policies typically involved an indifference to—perhaps even an ignorance of—what was actually being done to democratic, accountable government in the name of cost cutting and allegedly greater efficiency. It is one of the strengths of Shorrock's study that he goes into detail on Clinton's contributions to the wholesale privatization of our government, and of the intelligence agencies in particular.

Reagan launched his campaign to shrink the size of government and offer a large share of public expenditures to the private sector with the creation in 1982 of the "Private Sector Survey on Cost Control." In charge of the survey, which became known as the Grace Commission, he named the conservative businessman J. Peter Grace Jr., chairman of the W. R. Grace Corporation, one of the world's largest chemical companies—notorious for its production of asbestos and its involvement in numerous antipollution suits. The Grace company also had a long history of investment in Latin America, and Peter Grace was deeply committed to undercutting what he saw as leftist unions, particularly because they often favored state-led economic development.

The Grace Commission's actual achievements were modest. Its biggest success was undoubtedly the 1987 privatization of Conrail, the freight railroad for the northeastern states. Nothing much else happened on this front during the first Bush's administration, but Bill Clinton returned to privatization with a vengeance.

According to Shorrock:

> Bill Clinton . . . picked up the cudgel where the conservative Ronald Reagan left off and . . . took it deep into services once considered inherently governmental, including high-risk military operations and intelligence functions once reserved only for government agencies. By the end of [Clinton's first] term, more than 100,000 Pentagon jobs had been transferred to companies in the private sector—among them thousands of jobs in intelligence. . . . By the end of [his second] term in 2001, the administration had cut 360,000 jobs from the federal payroll and the government was spending 44 percent more on contractors than it had in 1993.

These activities were greatly abetted by the fact that the Republicans had gained control of the House of Representatives in 1994 for the first time in forty-three years. One liberal journalist described "outsourcing as a virtual joint venture between [House Majority Leader Newt] Gingrich and Clinton." The right-wing Heritage Foundation aptly labeled Clinton's 1996 budget as the "boldest privatization agenda put forth by any president to date."

After 2001, Bush and Cheney added an ideological rationale to the process Clinton had already launched so efficiently. They were enthusiastic supporters of "a neoconservative drive to siphon U.S.

spending on defense, national security, and social programs to large corporations friendly to the Bush administration."

THE PRIVATIZATION—AND
LOSS—OF INSTITUTIONAL MEMORY

The end result is what we see today: a government hollowed out in terms of military and intelligence functions. The KBR Corporation, for example, supplies food, laundry, and other personal services to our troops in Iraq and Afghanistan based on extremely lucrative no-bid contracts, while Blackwater Worldwide supplies security and analytical services to the CIA and the State Department in Baghdad. (Among other things, its armed mercenaries opened fire on, and killed, seventeen unarmed civilians in Nisour Square, Baghdad, on September 16, 2007, without any provocation, according to U.S. military reports.) The costs—both financial and personal—of privatization in the armed services and the intelligence community far exceed any alleged savings, and some of the consequences for democratic governance may prove irreparable.

These consequences include the sacrifice of professionalism within our intelligence services; the readiness of private contractors to engage in illegal activities without compunction and with impunity; the inability of Congress or citizens to carry out effective oversight of privately managed intelligence activities because of the wall of secrecy that surrounds them; and, perhaps most serious of all, the loss of the most valuable asset any intelligence organization possesses—its institutional memory.

Most of these consequences are obvious, even if almost never commented on by our politicians or paid much attention in the mainstream media. After all, the standards of a career CIA officer are very different from those of a corporate executive who must keep his eye on the contract he is fulfilling and future contracts that will determine the viability of his firm. The essence of professionalism for a career intelligence analyst is his integrity in laying out what the U.S. government should know about a foreign policy issue, regardless of the political interests of, or the costs to, the major players.

The loss of such professionalism within the CIA was starkly revealed in the 2002 National Intelligence Estimate on Iraq's possession of weapons of mass destruction. It still seems astonishing that no senior official, beginning with Secretary of State Colin Powell, saw fit to resign when the true dimensions of our intelligence failure became clear, least of all Director of Central Intelligence George Tenet.

A willingness to engage in activities ranging from the dubious to the outright felonious seems even more prevalent among our intelligence contractors than among the agencies themselves, and much harder for an outsider to detect. For example, following 9/11, Rear Admiral John Poindexter, then working for the Defense Advanced Research Projects Agency (DARPA) of the Department of Defense, got the bright idea that DARPA should start compiling dossiers on as many American citizens as possible in order to see whether "data-mining" procedures might reveal patterns of behavior associated with terrorist activities.

On November 14, 2002, the *New York Times* published a column by William Safire entitled "You Are a Suspect" in which he revealed that DARPA had been given a $200 million budget to compile dossiers on 300 million Americans. He wrote, "Every purchase you make with a credit card, every magazine subscription you buy and medical prescription you fill, every web site you visit and every e-mail you send or receive, every bank deposit you make, every trip you book, and every event you attend—all these transactions and communications will go into what the Defense

Department describes as a 'virtual centralized grand database.'"
This struck many members of Congress as too close to the
practices of the Gestapo and the Stasi under German totalitarianism, and so, the following year, they voted to defund the project.

However, Congress's action did not end the "total information awareness" program. The National Security Agency secretly
decided to continue it through its private contractors. The NSA
easily persuaded SAIC and Booz Allen Hamilton to carry on
with what Congress had declared to be a violation of the privacy
rights of the American public—for a price. As far as we know,
Admiral Poindexter's "Total Information Awareness Program" is
still going strong today.

The most serious immediate consequence of the privatization
of official governmental activities is the loss of institutional memory by our government's most sensitive organizations and agencies. Shorrock concludes, "So many former intelligence officers
joined the private sector [during the 1990s] that, by the turn of the
century, the institutional memory of the United States intelligence community now resides in the private sector. That's pretty
much where things stood on September 11, 2001."

This means that the CIA, the DIA, the NSA, and the other thirteen agencies in the U.S. intelligence community cannot easily be
reformed because their staffs have largely forgotten what they are
supposed to do, or how to go about it. They have not been drilled
and disciplined in the techniques, unexpected outcomes, and
know-how of previous projects, successful and failed.

As numerous studies have by now made clear, the abject failure of the American occupation of Iraq came about in significant
measure because the Department of Defense sent a remarkably
privatized military filled with incompetent amateurs to Baghdad
to administer the running of a defeated country. Defense Secretary
Robert M. Gates (a former director of the CIA) has repeatedly

warned that the United States is turning over far too many functions to the military because of its hollowing out of the Department of State and the Agency for International Development since the end of the Cold War. Gates believes that we are witnessing a "creeping militarization" of foreign policy—and, though this generally goes unsaid, both the military and the intelligence services have turned over far too many of their tasks to private companies and mercenaries.

When even Robert Gates begins to sound like President Eisenhower, it is time for ordinary citizens to pay attention. In my 2006 book *Nemesis: The Last Days of the American Republic*, with an eye to bringing the imperial presidency under some modest control, I advocated that we Americans abolish the CIA altogether, along with other dangerous and redundant agencies in our alphabet soup of sixteen secret intelligence agencies, and replace them with the State Department's professional staff devoted to collecting and analyzing foreign intelligence. I still hold that position.

Nonetheless, the current situation represents the worst of all possible worlds. Successive administrations and Congresses have made no effort to alter the CIA's role as the president's private army, even as we have increased its incompetence by turning over many of its functions to the private sector. We have thereby heightened the risks of war by accident, or by presidential whim, as well as of surprise attack because our government is no longer capable of accurately assessing what is going on in the world and because its intelligence agencies are so open to pressure, penetration, and manipulation of every kind.

PART III

BASEWORLD

8

AMERICA'S EMPIRE OF BASES

January 15, 2004

As distinct from other peoples, most Americans do not recognize—or do not want to recognize—that the United States dominates the world through its military power. Due to government secrecy, our citizens are often ignorant of the fact that our garrisons encircle the planet. This vast network of American bases on every continent except Antarctica actually constitutes a new form of empire—an empire of bases with its own geography not likely to be taught in any high school geography class. Without grasping the dimensions of this globe-girdling Baseworld, one can't begin to understand the size and nature of our imperial aspirations or the degree to which a new kind of militarism is undermining our constitutional order.

Our military deploys well over half a million soldiers, spies, technicians, teachers, dependents, and civilian contractors in other nations. To dominate the oceans and seas of the world, we have created some eleven naval task forces built around aircraft carriers whose names sum up our martial heritage—*Kitty Hawk, Enterprise, Nimitz, Dwight D. Eisenhower, Carl Vinson, Theodore*

Roosevelt, Abraham Lincoln, George Washington, John C. Stennis, Harry S. Truman, and *Ronald Reagan.** We operate numerous secret bases outside our territory to monitor what the people of the world, including our own citizens, are saying, faxing, or e-mailing to one another.

Our installations abroad bring profits to civilian industries, which design and manufacture weapons for the armed forces or, like the now well-publicized Kellogg, Brown & Root company, a subsidiary of the Halliburton Corporation of Houston, undertake contract services to build and maintain our far-flung outposts. One task of such contractors is to keep uniformed members of the imperium housed in comfortable quarters, well fed, amused, and supplied with enjoyable, affordable vacation facilities. Whole sectors of the American economy have come to rely on the military for sales. On the eve of our second war on Iraq, for example, while the Defense Department was ordering up an extra ration of cruise missiles and depleted-uranium armor-piercing tank shells, it also acquired 273,000 bottles of Native Tan sunblock, almost triple its 1999 order and undoubtedly a boon to the supplier, Control Supply Company of Tulsa, Oklahoma, and its subcontractor, Sun Fun Products of Daytona Beach, Florida.

AT LEAST SEVEN HUNDRED FOREIGN BASES

It's not easy to assess the size or exact value of our empire of bases. Official records on these subjects are misleading, although

---

* In 2009 the *Kitty Hawk* was decommissioned and the 97,000-ton aircraft carrier USS *George H. W. Bush*, named for the forty-first president, officially joined the U.S. Navy fleet. As of November 2009, the Navy had ten active Nimitz-class aircraft carriers, including the *George H. W. Bush*, and one slightly longer and lighter Enterprise-class carrier.

instructive. According to the Defense Department's annual "Base Structure Report" for fiscal year 2003, which itemizes foreign and domestic U.S. military real estate, the Pentagon currently owns or rents 702 overseas bases in about 130 countries and has another 6,000 bases in the United States and its territories. Pentagon bureaucrats calculate that it would require at least $113.2 billion to replace just the foreign bases—surely far too low a figure, but still larger than the gross domestic product of most countries—and an estimated $591.5 billion to replace all of them. The military high command deploys to our overseas bases some 253,288 uniformed personnel, plus an equal number of dependents and Department of Defense civilian officials, and employs an additional 44,446 locally hired foreigners. The Pentagon claims that these bases contain 44,870 barracks, hangars, hospitals, and other buildings that it owns, and that it leases 4,844 more.

These numbers, although staggeringly large, do not begin to cover all the actual bases we occupy globally. The 2003 Base Structure Report fails to mention, for instance, any garrisons in Kosovo—even though it is the site of the huge Camp Bondsteel, built in 1999 and maintained ever since by Kellogg, Brown & Root. The report similarly omits bases in Afghanistan, Iraq, Israel, Kuwait, Kyrgyzstan, Qatar, and Uzbekistan, although the U.S. military has established colossal base structures throughout the so-called arc of instability in the years since 9/11.

For Okinawa, the southernmost island of Japan, which has been an American military colony for the past fifty-eight years, the report deceptively lists only one Marine base, Camp Butler, when in fact Okinawa "hosts" ten Marine Corps bases, including Marine Corps Air Station Futenma occupying 1,186 acres in the center of that modest-sized island's second largest city. (Manhattan's Central Park, by contrast, is only 843 acres.) The Pentagon similarly fails to note all of the $5 billion worth of military and espionage installations in Britain, which have long been conveniently disguised as Royal Air Force bases. If there were an honest count, the actual size of our military empire would probably top a thousand different bases in other people's countries, but no one—possibly not even the Pentagon—knows the exact number for sure, although it has been distinctly on the rise in recent years.

For their occupants, these are not unpleasant places to live and work. Military service today, which is voluntary, bears almost no relation to the duties of a soldier during World War II or the Korean or Vietnam wars. Most chores like laundry, KP ("kitchen police"), mail call, and cleaning latrines have been subcontracted to private military companies such as Kellogg, Brown & Root, DynCorp, and the Vinnell Corporation. Fully one-third of the funds appropriated for the war in Iraq, for instance, are going into private American hands for exactly such services. Where possible, everything is done to make daily existence seem like a Hollywood version of life at home. According to the *Washington Post*, in Fallujah, just west of Baghdad, waiters in white shirts, black pants, and black bow ties serve dinner to the officers of the 82nd Airborne Division in their heavily guarded compound, and the first Burger King has already gone up inside the enormous military base we've established at Baghdad International Airport.

Some of these bases are so gigantic that they require as many as nine internal bus routes for soldiers and civilian contractors to get around inside the earthen berms and concertina wire. That's the case at Camp Anaconda, headquarters of the 3rd Brigade, 4th Infantry Division, whose job is to police some 1,500 square miles of Iraq north of Baghdad, from Samarra to Taji. Anaconda occupies 25 square kilometers and will ultimately house as many as 20,000 troops. Despite extensive security precautions, the base has frequently come under mortar attack, notably on the Fourth of July 2003, just as Arnold Schwarzenegger was chatting up our wounded at the local field hospital.

The military prefers bases that resemble small fundamentalist owns in the Bible Belt rather than the big population centers of he United States. For example, even though more than 100,000 women live on our overseas bases—including women in the services, spouses, and relatives of military personnel—obtaining an abortion at a local military hospital is prohibited. Since there are some 14,000 sexual assaults or attempted sexual assaults each year in the military, women who become pregnant overseas and want an abortion have no choice but to try the local economy, which cannot be either easy or pleasant in Baghdad or other parts of our empire these days.

Our armed missionaries live in a closed-off, self-contained world serviced by its own airline—the Air Mobility Command, with its fleet of long-range C-17 Globemasters, C-5 Galaxies, C-141 Starlifters, KC-135 Stratotankers, KC-10 Extenders, and C-9 Nightingales that link our far-flung outposts from Greenland to Australia. For generals and admirals, the military provides 71 Learjets, 13 Gulfstream IIIs, and 17 Cessna Citation luxury jets to fly them to such spots as the armed forces' ski and vacation center at Garmisch in the Bavarian Alps or to any of the 234 military golf courses the Pentagon operates worldwide. Defense Secretary Donald Rumsfeld flies around in his own personal Boeing 757, called a C-32A in the Air Force.

OUR "FOOTPRINT" ON THE WORLD

Of all the insensitive, if graphic, metaphors we've allowed into our vocabulary, none quite equals "footprint" to describe the military impact of our empire. Chairman of the Joint Chiefs of Staff General Richard Myers and senior members of the Senate's

Military Construction Subcommittee such as Dianne Feinstein (D-CA) are apparently incapable of completing a sentence without using it. Establishing a more impressive footprint has become part of the new justification for a major enlargement of our empire—and an announced repositioning of our bases and forces abroad—in the wake of our conquest of Iraq. The man in charge of this project was Andy Hoehn, deputy assistant secretary of defense for strategy. He and his colleagues were supposed to draw up plans to implement President Bush's preventive war strategy against "rogue states," "bad guys," and "evildoers." They identified something they called the arc of instability, which was said to run from the Andean region of South America (read: Colombia) through North Africa and then sweep across the Middle East to the Philippines and Indonesia. This was, of course, more or less identical with what used to be called the Third World—and perhaps no less crucially it covered the world's key oil reserves. Hoehn contended, "When you overlay our footprint onto that, we don't look particularly well positioned to deal with the problems we're now going to confront."

Once upon a time, you could trace the spread of imperialism by counting up colonies. America's version of the colony is the military base. By following the changing politics of global basing, one can learn much about our ever larger imperial stance and the militarism that grows with it. Militarism and imperialism are Siamese twins joined at the hip. Each thrives off the other. Already highly advanced in our country, they are both on the verge of a quantum leap that will almost surely stretch our military beyond its capabilities, bringing about fiscal insolvency and very possibly doing mortal damage to our republican institutions. The only way this is discussed in our press is via reportage on highly arcane plans for changes in basing policy and the positioning of troops abroad—and these plans, as reported in the media, cannot be taken at face value.

Marine Brig. Gen. Mastin Robeson, commanding our 1,800 troops occupying the old French Foreign Legion base at Camp Lemonier in Djibouti at the entrance to the Red Sea, claimed that in order to put "preventive war" into action, we require a "global presence," by which he meant gaining hegemony over any place that is not already under our thumb. According to the right-wing American Enterprise Institute, the idea is to create "a global cavalry" that can ride in from "frontier stockades" and shoot up the "bad guys" as soon as we get some intelligence on them.

"LILY PADS" IN AUSTRALIA, ROMANIA, MALI, ALGERIA . . .

In order to put our forces close to every hot spot or danger area in this newly discovered arc of instability, the Pentagon has been proposing—this is usually called "repositioning"—many new bases, including at least four and perhaps as many as six permanent ones in Iraq. A number of these are already under construction—at Baghdad International Airport, Tallil Air Base near Nasariyah, in the western desert near the Syrian border, and at Bashur airfield in the Kurdish region of the north. (This does not count the previously mentioned Anaconda, which is currently being called an "operating base," though it may very well become permanent over time.) In addition, we plan to keep under our control the whole northern quarter of Kuwait—1,600 of Kuwait's 6,900 square miles—that we used to resupply our Iraq legions and as a place for Green Zone bureaucrats to relax.

Other countries mentioned as sites for what Colin Powell called our new "family of bases": in the impoverished areas of the "new" Europe—Romania, Poland, and Bulgaria; in Asia—Pakistan (where we already have four bases), India, Australia, Singapore, Malaysia, the Philippines, and even, unbelievably, Vietnam; in North Africa—Morocco, Tunisia, and especially Algeria (scene of the slaughter of some 100,000 civilians since 1992, when, to quash an election, the military took over, backed by our country and France); and in West Africa—Senegal, Ghana, Mali, and Sierra Leone (even though it has been torn by civil war since 1991). The models for all these new installations, according to Pentagon sources, are the string of bases we have built around the Persian Gulf in the last two decades in such antidemocratic autocracies as Bahrain, Kuwait, Qatar, Oman, and the United Arab Emirates.

Most of these new bases will be what the military, in a switch of metaphors, calls "lily pads," to which our troops could jump like so many well-armed frogs from the homeland, our remaining NATO bases, or bases in the docile satellites of Japan and Britain. To offset the expense involved in such expansion, the Pentagon has leaked plans to close many of the huge Cold War military reservations in Germany, South Korea, and perhaps Okinawa as part of Secretary of Defense Rumsfeld's "rationalization" of our armed forces. In the wake of the Iraq victory, the United States has already withdrawn virtually all of its forces from Saudi Arabia and Turkey, partially as a way of punishing them for not supporting the war strongly enough. It wants to do the same thing to South Korea, perhaps the most anti-American democracy on earth today, which would free up the 2nd Infantry Division on the demilitarized zone with North Korea for probable deployment to the Middle East.

In Europe, these plans include giving up several bases in Germany, also in part because of Chancellor Gerhard Schröder's domestically popular defiance of Bush over Iraq. But the degree to which we are capable of doing so may prove limited indeed. At the simplest level, the Pentagon's planners do not really seem to grasp just how many buildings the 71,702 soldiers and airmen in Germany alone occupy and how expensive it would be to reposition most of them and build even slightly comparable bases, together with the necessary infrastructure, in former communist countries like Romania, one of Europe's poorest countries. Lt. Col. Amy Ehmann in Hanau, Germany, has said to the press "There's no place to put these people" in Romania, Bulgaria, or Djibouti, and she predicts that 80 percent of them will in the end stay in Germany. It's also certain that generals of the high command have no intention of living in backwaters like Constanta, Romania, and will keep the U.S. military headquarters in Stuttgart while holding on to Ramstein Air Force Base, Spangdahlem Air Force Base, and the Grafenwöhr Training Area.

One reason why the Pentagon is considering moving out of rich democracies like Germany and South Korea and looks covetously at military dictatorships and poverty-stricken dependencies is to take advantage of what the Pentagon calls their "more permissive environmental regulations." The Pentagon always imposes on countries in which it deploys our forces so-called Status of Forces Agreements, which usually exempt the United States from cleaning up or paying for the environmental damage it causes. This is a standing grievance in Okinawa, where the American environmental record has been nothing short of abominable. Part of this attitude is simply the desire of the Pentagon to put itself beyond any of the restraints that govern civilian life, an attitude increasingly at play in the "homeland" as well. For example, the 2004 defense authorization bill of $401.3 billion that President Bush signed into law in November 2003 exempted the military from abiding by the Endangered Species Act and the Marine Mammal Protection Act.

While there is every reason to believe that the impulse to create ever more lily pads in the Third World remains unchecked, there are several reasons to doubt that some of the more grandiose plans, for either expansion or downsizing, will ever be put into effect or, if they are, that they will do anything other than make the problem of terrorism worse than it is. For one thing, Russia is opposed to the expansion of U.S. military power on its borders and is already moving to checkmate American basing sorties into places such as Georgia, Kyrgyzstan, and Uzbekistan. The first post-Soviet-era Russian airbase in Kyrgyzstan has just been completed forty miles from the U.S. base at Bishkek, and in December 2003 the dictator of Uzbekistan, Islam Karimov, declared that he would not permit a permanent deployment of U.S. forces in his country, even though we already have a base there.

When it comes to downsizing, on the other hand, domestic politics comes into play. As an efficiency measure, Secretary of Defense Rumsfeld has said he'd like to be rid of at least one-third of domestic Army bases and one-quarter of domestic Air Force bases, a guaranteed political firestorm on Capitol Hill. In order to protect their respective states' bases, the two mother hens of the Senate's Military Construction Appropriations Subcommittee, Kay Bailey Hutchison (R-TX) and Dianne Feinstein, demanded that the Pentagon close overseas bases first and bring the troops now stationed there home to domestic bases, which could then remain open. Hutchison and Feinstein included in the Military Appropriations Act of 2004 money for an independent commission to investigate and report on overseas bases that are no longer needed. The Bush administration opposed this provision of the act, but it passed anyway, and the president signed it into law on November 22, 2003. The Pentagon is probably adept enough to hamstring the commission, but a domestic base-closing furor always looms on the horizon.

By far the greatest defect in the "global cavalry" strategy, however, is that it accentuates Washington's impulse to apply irrelevant military remedies to terrorism. As the prominent British military historian Correlli Barnett has observed, the U.S. attacks on Afghanistan and Iraq only increased the threat of al-Qaeda. From 1993 through the 9/11 assaults of 2001, there were five major al-Qaeda attacks worldwide; in the two years since then there have been seventeen such bombings, including the Istanbul suicide assaults on the British consulate and an HSBC Bank. Military operations against terrorists are not the solution. As Barnett puts it, "Rather than kicking down front doors and barging into ancient and complex societies with simple nostrums of 'freedom and democracy,' we need tactics of cunning and subtlety, based on a profound understanding of the people and cultures we are dealing with—an understanding up till now entirely lacking in the top-level policy-makers in Washington, especially in the Pentagon."

In his notorious "long, hard slog" memo on Iraq of October 16, 2003, Defense Secretary Rumsfeld wrote, "Today, we lack metrics to know if we are winning or losing the global war on terror." Barnett's "metrics" indicate otherwise. But the war on terror is at best only a small part of the reason for all our military strategizing. The real reason for constructing this new ring of American bases along the equator is to expand our empire and reinforce our military domination of the world.

9

AMERICA'S UNWELCOME ADVANCES

August 22, 2008

Imperialism, meaning militarily stronger nations dominating and exploiting weaker ones, has been a prominent feature of the international system for several centuries, but it may be coming to an end. Overwhelming majorities in numerous countries now condemn it—with the possible exception of some observers who believe it promotes "stability" and some United States politicians who still vigorously debate the pros and cons of America's continuing military hegemony over much of the globe.

Imperialism's current decline began in 1991 with the disintegration of the former Soviet Union and the collapse of its empire. The United States now seems to be the last of a dying species—the sole remaining multinational empire. (There are only a few vestiges of the old Dutch, English, and French empires, mostly in the form of island colonies and other enclaves in and around the Caribbean.) As the wars in Iraq and Afghanistan have made clear, the United States is increasingly stressed by the demands of maintaining its empire through its own military resources. Change is in the air.

According to the Pentagon's 2008 "Base Structure Report," its annual unclassified inventory of the real estate it owns or leases around the world, the United States maintains 761 active military "sites" in foreign countries. (That's the Defense Department's preferred term, rather than "bases," although bases are what they are.) Counting domestic military bases and those on U.S. territories, the total is 5,429.

The overseas figure fluctuates year to year. The 2008 total is down from 823 in the Pentagon's 2007 report, but the 2007 number was up from 766 in 2006. The current total is, however, substantially less than the Cold War peak of 1,014 in 1967. Still, given that there are only 192 countries in the United Nations, 761 foreign bases is a remarkable example of imperial overstretch—even more so considering that official military reports understate the actual size of the U.S. footprint. (The official figures omit espionage bases, those located in war zones, including Iraq and Afghanistan, and miscellaneous facilities in places considered too sensitive to discuss or which the Pentagon for its own reasons chooses to exclude—e.g., in Israel, Kosovo, or Jordan.)

"The characteristic form of U.S. power outside its territory is not colonial, or indirect rule within a colonial framework of direct control, but a system of satellite or compliant states," observes Eric Hobsbawm, the British historian of modern empires. In this sense America behaves more like the Soviet empire in Europe after World War II than the British or French empires of the nineteenth century.

To garrison its empire, as of December 2007, the United States had 510,927 service personnel (including sailors afloat) deployed in 151 foreign countries.

The reach of the U.S. military expanded rapidly after World War II and the Korean truce, when we acquired our largest overseas enclaves in the defeated countries of Germany, Italy, and Japan, and on Allied turf in Great Britain and South Korea. But despite the wartime origins of many overseas bases, they have little to do with our national security. America does not necessarily need forward-deployed military forces to engage in either offensive or defensive operations, because domestic bases are more than sufficient for those purposes. The Air Force can shuttle troops and equipment or launch bombers from continental American bases using aerial refueling, which has been standard Strategic Air Command doctrine and practice since 1951. Only after the Cold War was well under way did the Strategic Air Command expand into several overseas bases in Canada, England, Greenland, Japan, Oman, Spain, and Thailand in an effort to complicate Soviet retaliatory strategy.

We also project power through our fleet of strategic submarines, armed with either nuclear-tipped or conventional high-explosive ballistic missiles, and some eleven naval task forces built around nuclear-powered aircraft carriers. With these floating bases dominating the seas, we need not interfere with other nations' sovereignty by forcing land bases upon them.

In fact, the purpose of our overseas bases is to maintain U.S. dominance in the world, and to reinforce what military analyst Charles Maier calls our "empire of consumption." The United States possesses less than 5 percent of global population but consumes about one-quarter of all global resources, including petroleum. Our empire exists so we can exploit a much greater share of the world's wealth than we are entitled to, and so we can prevent other nations from combining against us to take their rightful share.

Some nations have, however, started to balk at America's military presence. Thanks to the policies of the Bush administration, large majorities in numerous countries are now strongly anti-American. In June 2008, a House Foreign Affairs subcommittee issued a report titled *The Decline in America's Reputation: Why?* It blamed falling approval ratings abroad on the Iraq War, our support for repressive governments, a perception of U.S. bias in the Israeli-Palestinian dispute, and the "torture and abuse of prisoners." The result: a growing number of foreign protest movements objecting to the presence of American troops and their families, mercenaries, and spies.

The most serious erosion of American power appears to be occurring in Latin America, where a majority of countries either actively detest us—particularly Venezuela, Bolivia, Ecuador, and Cuba—or are hostile to our economic policies. Most have been distrustful ever since it was revealed that the United States stood behind the late-twentieth-century tortures, disappearances, death squads, military coups, and right-wing pogroms against workers, peasants, and the educated in such countries as Argentina, Brazil, Chile, Guatemala, Nicaragua, Panama, and Uruguay. The citizens of Paraguay appear to be recent converts to anti-Americanism thanks to speculation that the United States is trying to establish a military presence there. The only places where American troops are still more or less welcome in Latin America are Colombia, El Salvador, Honduras, and, tentatively, Peru, plus a few European colonial outposts in the Caribbean.

In Ecuador, the primary battleground has been Eloy Alfaro Air Base, located next door to Manta, Ecuador's most important Pacific seaport. In 1999, claiming to be interested only in interrupting the narcotics traffic and assisting the local population, the U.S. military obtained a ten-year deal to use the airfield and then, after 9/11, turned it into a major hub for counterinsurgency, anti-immigrant activities, and espionage. Ecuadoreans are convinced that the Americans based at Manta provided the intelligence that enabled Colombian forces to launch a March 2008 cross-border attack, killing twenty-one Colombian insurgents on Ecuador's turf.

In 2006, newly elected Ecuadorian president Rafael Correa declared that he wouldn't renew the American lease when it expires in November 2009—unless, he tauntingly proposed the following year, the United States would let Ecuador have a base in Miami. Correa has since offered to lease the air base to the Chinese for commercial use. Ecuador also rejected a U.S. bid to set up a base on the island of Baltra in the Galápagos, a protected wildlife refuge. The 180 U.S. soldiers and several hundred contractors at Manta have since found a new home in Colombia.

Peru has proved problematic for the Pentagon. In July 2008, the United States sent close to a thousand soldiers to "dig wells and do public health work" in the southern Ayacucho region, an area once controlled by the Shining Path guerrillas. The U.S. deployment, while seemingly harmless, has provoked demonstrations in many Peruvian cities, where such "friendship" missions are viewed as a pretext for an expanded U.S. military presence. There is an airfield in Ayacucho—Los Cabitos—that the Americans would like to occupy, as it might provide easy access to Bolivia and Colombia.

The United States faces popular protests against its bases in numerous other countries. Disputes over military pollution and the handling of soldiers suspected of crimes have led to widespread resentment of U.S. troop presence in South Korea and the Japanese prefecture of Okinawa. Meanwhile, in Italy, where the United States still has at least eighty-three military installations, demonstrations erupted in 2006 when it was revealed that the government would let the U.S. Army greatly enlarge its base in the northern city of Vicenza.

A town of about 120,000 nestled midway between Venice and Verona, Vicenza was home and showplace of the renowned Renaissance architect Andrea Palladio, whose work so impressed Thomas Jefferson that he incorporated Palladian themes into his plantation at Monticello and the Rotunda at the University of Virginia. Vicenza already housed six thousand U.S. troops when, in late 2003, U.S. officials began secretly negotiating to bring in four more Army battalions from Germany. The Americans proposed closing Vicenza's small municipal airport at Dal Molin, across town from the existing base, so they could build barracks and other facilities at the airport for 1,750 additional troops.

But locals still haven't forgotten the 1998 incident in which a Marine pilot from nearby Aviano Air Base severed an Italian gondola cable with his jet, killing twenty skiers. The pilot, who'd been flying his Prowler faster and lower than Pentagon regulations permit, was later acquitted by a U.S. military court, although he did serve five months in prison for destroying evidence in the form of a cockpit video. Local opposition to the Vicenza proposal led judges to suspend work at Dal Molin in June 2008, leading to a standoff with the Berlusconi government, which supports the base expansion. A month later, the Council of State, Italy's highest court, overturned the local decision, declaring that "the authorization of a military base is the exclusive competency of the state."

Similar disputes are unfolding in Poland, the Czech Republic, South Korea, and Japan. For several years the Pentagon has been negotiating with the Polish and Czech governments to build bases in their countries for radar tracking and missile launching sites as part of its proposed anti-ICBM (Intercontinental Ballistic Missile) network against an alleged threat from Iran. Russia, however, does not accept the U.S. explanation and believes these bases are aimed at it. In July 2008, Secretary of State Condoleezza Rice successfully concluded a missile defense deal with the Czech government, but it required ratification by the parliament, with two-thirds of the population said to be opposed. While the Polish government had been slow to sign on, Russia's attack on Georgia appeared to change its attitude. In light of Russian assertiveness, the Poles quickly accepted the American proposal to base antimissile missiles on their soil.

In South Korea, America faces massive protests over its attempt to construct new headquarters at Pyeongtaek, some forty miles south of Seoul, where it hopes to locate 17,000 troops and associated civilians, for a total of 43,000 people. Pyeongtaek would replace the Yongsan Garrison, the old Japanese headquarters in central Seoul that U.S. troops have occupied since 1945.

Meanwhile, the United States and Japan are locked in a perennial dispute over the $1.86 billion Japan pays annually to support U.S. troops and their families on the main islands of Japan and Okinawa. The Japanese call this the "sympathy budget" in an expression of cynicism over the fact that the United States cannot seem to afford its own foreign policy. The Americans want Japan to pay more, but the Japanese have balked.

All overseas U.S. bases create tensions with the people forced to live in their shadow, but one of the most shameful examples involves the Indian Ocean island of Diego Garcia. During the 1960s, the United States leased the island from Great Britain, which, on behalf of its new tenant, forcibly expelled the entire indigenous population, relocating the islanders some 1,200 miles away in Mauritius and the Seychelles.

Diego Garcia remains a U.S. naval and bomber base, espionage center, secret CIA prison, and transit point for prisoners en route to harsh interrogation at Guantánamo Bay and elsewhere. It has an anchorage for some twenty ships, a nuclear weapons storage facility, a 12,000-foot runway, and accommodations and amenities for 5,200 Americans and fifty British police. According to many sources, including retired general Barry McCaffrey, the base was used after 9/11 as a prison (called Camp Justice) for high-value detainees from the Afghan and Iraq wars.

Perhaps one sign of trouble brewing for America's overseas enclaves has been the world's condemnation of its long-term ambitions in Iraq. In June 2008, it was revealed that the United States was secretly pressing Iraq to let it retain some fifty-eight bases on Iraqi soil indefinitely, plus other concessions that would make Iraq a long-term dependency of the United States. The negotiations over a long-term American presence were a debacle for the rule of law and what's left of America's reputation, even though the lame-duck Bush administration backed down from its more outrageous demands in the end.

Like all empires of the past, the American version of empire is destined to come to an end, either voluntarily or of necessity. When that will occur is impossible to foretell, but the pressures of America's massive indebtedness, the growing contradiction between the needs of its civilian economy and its military-industrial complex, and its dependence on a volunteer army and innumerable private contractors strongly indicate an empire built on fragile foundations. Over the next few years, resistance to military overtures is likely to grow, meaning the agenda of national politics will be increasingly dominated by issues of empire liquidation—peacefully or otherwise.

UPDATE 2010

According to the Defense Department's Base Structure Report for fiscal year 2009, the Pentagon owned or rented 716 overseas bases and another 4,863 in the United States and its territories. Pentagon bureaucrats calculate that it would require at least $124.2 billion to replace just the foreign bases and an estimated $720 billion to replace all of them.

Like earlier Base Structure Reports, the 2009 edition failed to mention any garrisons in the Iraq and Afghan war zones, as well as any bases or facilities used in countries such as Jordan and Qatar. By the summer of 2009, for example, there were still nearly three hundred U.S. bases and outposts in Iraq, with the number set to drop to fifty or fewer by August 31, 2010—President Obama's deadline for removing combat troops from the country. However, that target date and a stated intention to remove all U.S. forces by the end of 2011 were seemingly abrogated months later by his secretary of defense Robert Gates, who admitted, "I wouldn't be a bit surprised to see agreements between ourselves and the Iraqis that continues a train, equip and advise role beyond the end of 2011." As a result, don't count on U.S. bases necessarily disappearing from Iraq by 2012.

Elsewhere, bases continued to expand despite local opposition. In Afghanistan, a surge in base building meant that by early 2010, U.S. and coalition allies occupied nearly four hundred bases—from mega- to micro-sized—in the country, with more in the pipeline. In September 2009, the last U.S. troops left Ecuador's Manta air base. Just months before, however, details emerged in the press of an agreement between the United States and Colombia to give Washington access to seven military bases in that country.

Despite protests by ordinary Italians as well as the mayor of Vicenza, Prime Minister Silvio Berlusconi has pushed ahead with the expansion of the U.S. base being built in that town, which is scheduled to be completed in 2011.

Only in Japan did real roadblocks to U.S. base expansion emerge. In 2009, the Japanese government announced that it was reconsidering a 2006 agreement with the Bush administration to relocate U.S. Marine Corps Air Station Futenma in Okinawa to a proposed airfield at Camp Schwab along the island's rural northeastern coast. Subsequently, relations between the two allies soured. Early in 2010, the fiftieth anniversary of the joint U.S.-Japanese Security Treaty allowing the large-scale U.S. presence in the country, Japan's new prime minister, Yukio Hatoyama, announced plans to press for a more open and equal relationship between the two nations, while his country also considered updating the agreement to make the United States responsible for the environmental cleanup of sites used by the U.S. military.

10

BASELESS EXPENDITURES

July 2, 2009

The U.S. Empire of Bases—at $102 billion a year, already the world's costliest military enterprise—just got a good deal more expensive. As a start, on May 27, 2009, we learned that the State Department will build a new "embassy" in Islamabad, Pakistan, which at $736 million will be the second priciest ever constructed, only $4 million less, if cost overruns don't occur, than the Vatican City–sized one the Bush administration put up in Baghdad. The State Department was also reportedly planning to buy the five-star Pearl Continental Hotel (complete with pool) in Peshawar, near the border with Afghanistan, to use as a consulate and living quarters for its staff there.

Unfortunately for such plans, on June 9, Pakistani militants rammed a truck filled with explosives into the hotel, killing eighteen occupants, wounding at least fifty-five, and collapsing one entire wing of the structure. There has been no news since about whether the State Department is going ahead with the purchase.

Whatever the costs turn out to be, they will not be included in our already bloated military budget, even though none of these structures is designed to be a true embassy—a place, that is, where local people come for visas and American officials represent the commercial and diplomatic interests of their country. Instead, these so-called embassies will actually be walled compounds, akin to medieval fortresses, where American spies, soldiers, intelligence officials, and diplomats try to keep an eye on hostile populations in a region at war. One can predict with certainty that they will house a large contingent of Marines and include rooftop helicopter pads for quick getaways.

While it may be comforting for State Department employees working in dangerous places to know that they have some physical protection, it must also be obvious to them, as well as to the people in the countries where they serve, that they will now be visibly part of an in-your-face American imperial presence. We shouldn't be surprised when militants attacking the United States find one of our baselike embassies, however heavily guarded, an easier target than a large military base.

And what is being done about those military bases anyway—now close to eight hundred of them dotted across the globe in other people's countries? Even as Congress and the Obama administration wrangle over the cost of bank bailouts, a new health plan, pollution controls, and other much-needed domestic expenditures, no one suggests that closing some of these unpopular, expensive imperial enclaves might be a good way to save some money.

Instead, they are evidently about to become even more expensive. On June 23, we learned that Kyrgyzstan, the former Central Asian Soviet republic that, back in February 2009, announced it was going to kick the U.S. military out of Manas Air Base (used since 2001 as a staging area for the Afghan War), has been persuaded to let us stay. But here's the catch: in return for doing us that favor, the annual rent Washington pays for use of the base will more than triple, from $17.4 million to $60 million, with millions more to go into promised improvements in airport facilities and other financial sweeteners. All this because the Obama administration, having committed itself to a widening war in the region, is convinced it needs this base to store and transship supplies to Afghanistan.

This development will probably not go unnoticed in other countries where Americans are also unpopular occupiers. For example, the Ecuadoreans have told us to leave Manta Air Base. Of course, they have their pride to consider, not to speak of the fact that they don't like American soldiers mucking about in Colombia and Peru. Nonetheless, they could probably use a spot more money.

And what about the Japanese who, for more than fifty-seven years, have been paying big bucks to host American bases on their soil? Recently, they reached a deal with Washington to move some American Marines from bases on Okinawa to the U.S. territory of Guam. In the process, however, they were forced to shell out not only for the cost of the Marines' removal, but also to build new facilities on Guam for their arrival. Is it possible that they will now take a cue from the government of Kyrgyzstan and just tell the Americans to get out and pay for it themselves? Or might they at least stop funding the same American military personnel who regularly rape Japanese women (at the rate of about two per month) and make life miserable for whoever lives near the thirty-eight U.S. bases on Okinawa? This is certainly what the Okinawans have been hoping and praying for ever since we arrived in 1945.

In fact, I have a suggestion for other countries that are getting a bit weary of the American military presence on their soil: cash in now, before it's too late. Either up the ante or tell the Americans to go home. I encourage this behavior because I'm convinced that the U.S. Empire of Bases will soon enough bankrupt our country, and so—on the analogy of a financial bubble or a pyramid scheme—if you're an investor, it's better to get your money out while you still can.

This is, of course, something that has occurred to the Chinese and other financiers of the American national debt. Only they're cashing in quietly and slowly in order not to tank the dollar while they're still holding on to such a bundle of them. Make no mistake, though: whether we're being bled rapidly or slowly, we are bleeding; and hanging on to our military empire and all the bases that go with it will ultimately spell the end of the United States as we know it.

Count on this: future generations of Americans traveling abroad decades from now won't find the landscape dotted with near-billion-dollar "embassies."

PART IV

THE PENTAGON

TAKES US DOWN

11

GOING BANKRUPT

January 22, 2008

The military adventurers of the Bush administration had much in common with the corporate leaders of the defunct energy company Enron. Both groups of men thought that they were "the smartest guys in the room," the title of Alex Gibney's prizewinning film on what went wrong at Enron. The neoconservatives in the White House and the Pentagon outsmarted themselves. They failed even to address the problem of how to finance their schemes of imperialist wars and global domination.

As a result, going into 2008, the United States found itself in the anomalous position of being unable to pay for its own elevated living standards or its wasteful, overly large military establishment. Its government no longer even attempted to reduce the ruinous expenses of maintaining huge standing armies, replacing the equipment that seven years of wars had destroyed or worn out, or preparing for a war in outer space against unknown adversaries. Instead, the Bush administration put off these costs for future generations to pay—or repudiate. This utter fiscal irresponsibility was disguised through many manipulative financial schemes (such as causing poorer countries to lend us unprecedented sums of money), but the time of reckoning is fast approaching.

There are three broad aspects to our debt crisis. First, we are spending insane amounts of money on "defense" projects that bear no relationship to the national security of the United States. Simultaneously, we are keeping the income tax burdens on the richest segments of the American population at strikingly low levels.

Second, we continue to believe that we can compensate for the accelerating erosion of our manufacturing base and our loss of jobs to foreign countries through massive military expenditures—so-called military Keynesianism. By "military Keynesianism," I mean the mistaken belief that public policies focused on frequent wars, huge expenditures on weapons and munitions, and large standing armies can indefinitely sustain a wealthy capitalist economy. The opposite is actually true.

Third, in our devotion to militarism (despite our limited resources), we are failing to invest in our social infrastructure and other requirements for the long-term health of our country. These are what economists call opportunity costs, things not done because we spent our money on something else. Our public education system has deteriorated alarmingly. We have failed to provide health care to all our citizens and neglected our responsibilities as the world's number one polluter. Most important, we have lost our competitiveness as a manufacturer for civilian needs—an infinitely more efficient use of scarce resources than arms manufacturing. Let me discuss each of these.

THE CURRENT FISCAL DISASTER

It is virtually impossible to overstate the profligacy of what our government spends on the military. The Department of Defense's planned expenditures for fiscal year 2008 were larger than all other nations' military budgets combined. The supplementary budget to pay for the wars in Iraq and Afghanistan, not part of the official defense budget, was itself larger than the combined military budgets of Russia and China. Defense-related spending for fiscal 2008 exceeded $1 trillion for the first time in history. The United States has become the largest single salesman of arms and munitions to other nations. Leaving out of account the two ongoing wars, defense spending has doubled since the mid-1990s. The defense budget for fiscal 2008 was the largest since World War II.

Before we try to break down and analyze this gargantuan sum, there is one important caveat. Figures on defense spending are notoriously unreliable. The numbers released by the Congressional Reference Service and the Congressional Budget Office do not agree with each other. Robert Higgs, senior fellow for political economy at the Independent Institute, says, "A well-founded rule of thumb is to take the Pentagon's (always well publicized) basic budget total and double it." Even a cursory reading of newspaper articles about the Department of Defense will turn up major differences in statistics about its expenses. Some 30 to 40 percent of the defense budget is "black," meaning that these sections contain hidden expenditures for classified projects. There is no possible way to know what they include or whether their total amounts are accurate.

There are many reasons for this budgetary sleight of hand—including a desire for secrecy on the part of the president, the secretary of defense, and the military-industrial complex—but the chief one is that members of Congress, who profit enormously from defense jobs and pork-barrel projects in their districts, have a political interest in supporting the Department of Defense. In 1996, in an attempt to bring accounting standards within the executive branch somewhat closer to those of the civilian economy, Congress passed the Federal Financial Management Improvement Act. It required all federal agencies to hire outside auditors to review their books and release the results to the public. Neither the Department of Defense nor the Department of Homeland Security has ever complied. Congress has complained but has not penalized either department for ignoring the law. The result is that all numbers released by the Pentagon should be regarded as suspect.

In discussing the fiscal 2008 defense budget, as released to the press on February 7, 2007, I have been guided by two experienced and reliable analysts: William D. Hartung of the New America Foundation's Arms and Security Initiative and Fred Kaplan, defense correspondent for Slate.org. They agree that the Department of Defense requested $481.4 billion for salaries, operations (except in Iraq and Afghanistan), and equipment. They also agree on a figure of $141.7 billion for the "supplemental" budget to fight the "global war on terrorism"—that is, the two ongoing wars that the general public may think are actually covered by the basic Pentagon budget. The Department of Defense also asked for an extra $93.4 billion to pay for hitherto unmentioned war costs in the remainder of 2007 and, most creatively, an additional "allowance" (a new term in defense budget documents) of $50 billion to be charged to fiscal year 2009. This comes to a total spending request by the Department of Defense of $766.5 billion.

But there is much more. In an attempt to disguise the true size of the American military empire, the government has long hidden major military-related expenditures in departments other than Defense. For example, $23.4 billion for the Department of Energy goes toward developing and maintaining nuclear warheads, and $25.3 billion in the Department of State budget is spent on foreign military assistance (primarily for Israel, Saudi

Arabia, Bahrain, Kuwait, Oman, Qatar, the United Arab Emirates, Egypt, and Pakistan). Another $1.03 billion outside the official Department of Defense budget is now needed for recruitment and reenlistment incentives for the overstretched U.S. military itself, up from a mere $174 million in 2003, the year the war in Iraq began. The Department of Veterans Affairs currently gets at least $75.7 billion, 50 percent of which goes for the long-term care of the grievously injured among the at least 28,870 soldiers so far wounded in Iraq and another 1,708 in Afghanistan. The amount is universally derided as inadequate. Another $46.4 billion goes to the Department of Homeland Security.

Missing as well from this compilation is $1.9 billion to the Department of Justice for the paramilitary activities of the FBI; $38.5 billion to the Department of the Treasury for the Military Retirement Fund; $7.6 billion for the military-related activities of the National Aeronautics and Space Administration; and well over $200 billion in interest for past debt-financed defense outlays. This brings U.S. spending for its military establishment during the fiscal year 2008, conservatively calculated, to at least $1.1 trillion.

MILITARY KEYNESIANISM

Such expenditures are not only morally obscene, they are fiscally unsustainable. Many neoconservatives and poorly informed patriotic Americans believe that even though our defense budget is huge, we can afford it because we are the richest country on earth. Unfortunately, that statement is no longer true. The world's richest political entity, according to the CIA's "World Factbook," is the European Union. The EU's 2006 GDP (gross domestic product—all goods and services produced domestically) was estimated to be slightly larger than that of the United

States. However, China's 2006 GDP was only slightly smaller than that of the United States, and Japan was the world's fourth richest nation.

A more telling comparison that reveals just how much worse we're doing can be found among the "current accounts" of various nations. The current account measures the net trade surplus or deficit of a country plus cross-border payments of interest, royalties, dividends, capital gains, foreign aid, and other income. For example, in order for Japan to manufacture anything, it must import all required raw materials. Even after this incredible expense is met, it still has an $88 billion per year trade surplus with the United States and enjoys the world's second-highest current account balance. (China is number one.) The United States, by contrast, is number 163—dead last on the list, worse than countries like Australia and the United Kingdom that also have large trade deficits. Its 2006 current account deficit was $811.5 billion; second-worst was Spain at $106.4 billion. This is what is unsustainable.

It's not just that our tastes for foreign goods, including imported oil, vastly exceed our ability to pay for them. We are financing them through massive borrowing. On November 7, 2007, the U.S. Treasury announced that the national debt had breached $9 trillion for the first time. This was just five weeks after Congress raised the so-called debt ceiling to $9.815 trillion. If you begin in 1789, at the moment the Constitution became the supreme law of the land, the debt accumulated by the federal government did not top $1 trillion until 1981. When George Bush became president in January 2001, it stood at approximately $5.7 trillion. Since then, it has increased by 45 percent. This huge debt can be largely explained by our defense expenditures in comparison with the rest of the world.

The world's top ten military spenders and the approximate

amounts each country currently budgets for its military establishment are:

1. United States (FY08 budget), $623 billion
2. China (2004), $65 billion
3. Russia, $50 billion
4. France (2005), $45 billion
5. United Kingdom, $42.8 billion
6. Japan (2007), $41.75 billion
7. Germany (2003), $35.1 billion
8. Italy (2003), $28.2 billion
9. South Korea (2003), $21.1 billion
10. India (2005 est.), $19 billion

World total military expenditures (2004 est.), $1,100 billion
World total (minus the United States), $500 billion

Our excessive military expenditures did not occur over just a few short years or simply because of the Bush administration's policies. They have been going on for a very long time in accordance with a superficially plausible ideology and have now become entrenched in our democratic political system, where they are starting to wreak havoc. This ideology I call military Keynesianism—the determination to maintain a permanent war economy and to treat military output as an ordinary economic product, even though it makes no contribution to either production or consumption.

This ideology goes back to the first years of the Cold War. During the late 1940s, the United States was haunted by economic anxieties. The Great Depression of the 1930s had been overcome only by the war production boom of World War II. With peace and demobilization, there was a pervasive fear that the Depression would return. During 1949, alarmed by the Soviet Union's detonation of an atomic bomb, the looming communist victory in the Chinese civil war, a domestic recession, and the lowering of the Iron Curtain around the USSR's European satellites, the United States sought to draft basic strategy for the emerging Cold War. The result was the militaristic National Security Council Report 68 (NSC-68) drafted under the supervision of Paul Nitze, then head of the Policy Planning Staff in the State Department. Dated April 14, 1950, and signed by President Harry S. Truman on September 30, 1950, it laid out the basic public economic policies that the United States pursues to the present day.

In its conclusions, NSC-68 asserted: "One of the most significant lessons of our World War II experience was that the American economy, when it operates at a level approaching full efficiency, can provide enormous resources for purposes other than civilian consumption while simultaneously providing a high standard of living."

With this understanding, American strategists began to build up a massive munitions industry, both to counter the military might of the Soviet Union (which they consistently overstated) and also to maintain full employment as well as ward off a possible return of the Depression. The result was that, under Pentagon leadership, entire new industries were created to manufacture large aircraft, nuclear-powered submarines, nuclear warheads, intercontinental ballistic missiles, and surveillance and communications satellites. This led to what President Eisenhower warned against in his farewell address of February 6, 1961: "The conjunction of an immense military establishment and a large arms industry is new in the American experience"—that is, the military-industrial complex.

By 1990, the value of the weapons, equipment, and factories devoted to the Department of Defense was 83 percent of the value of all plants and equipment in American manufacturing. From

1947 to 1990, the combined U.S. military budgets amounted to $8.7 trillion. Even though the Soviet Union no longer exists, U.S. reliance on military Keynesianism has, if anything, ratcheted up, thanks to the massive vested interests that have become entrenched around the military establishment. Over time, a commitment to both guns and butter has proven an unstable configuration. Military industries crowd out the civilian economy and lead to severe economic weaknesses. Devotion to military Keynesianism is, in fact, a form of slow economic suicide.

On May 1, 2007, the Center for Economic and Policy Research in Washington, D.C., released a study prepared by the global forecasting company Global Insight on the long-term economic impact of increased military spending. Guided by economist Dean Baker, this research showed that after an initial demand stimulus, by about the sixth year the effect of increased military spending turns negative. Needless to say, the U.S. economy has had to cope with growing defense spending for more than sixty years. He found that after ten years of higher defense spending, there would be 464,000 fewer jobs than in a baseline scenario that involved lower defense spending.

Baker concluded, "It is often believed that wars and military spending increases are good for the economy. In fact, most economic models show that military spending diverts resources from productive uses, such as consumption and investment, and ultimately slows economic growth and reduces employment."

These are only some of the many deleterious effects of military Keynesianism.

HOLLOWING OUT THE AMERICAN ECONOMY

It was believed that the United States could afford both a massive military establishment and a high standard of living, and that it needed both to maintain full employment. But it did not work out that way. By the 1960s, it was becoming apparent that turning over the nation's largest manufacturing enterprises to the Department of Defense and producing goods without any investment or consumption value was starting to crowd out civilian economic activities. The historian Thomas E. Woods Jr. observes that during the 1950s and 1960s, between one-third and two-thirds of all American research talent was siphoned off into the military sector. It is, of course, impossible to know what innovations never appeared as a result of this diversion of resources and brainpower into the service of the military, but it was during the 1960s that we first began to notice Japan was outpacing us in the design and quality of a range of consumer goods, including household electronics and automobiles.

Nuclear weapons furnish a striking illustration of these anomalies. Between the 1940s and 1996, the United States spent at least $5.8 trillion on the development, testing, and construction of nuclear bombs. By 1967, the peak year of its nuclear stockpile, the United States possessed some 32,500 deliverable atomic and hydrogen bombs, none of which, thankfully, was ever used. They perfectly illustrate the Keynesian principle that the government can provide make-work jobs to keep people employed. Nuclear weapons were not just America's secret weapon, but also its secret economic weapon. As of 2006, we still had 9,960 of them. There is today no sane use for them, while the trillions spent on them could have been used to solve the problems of Social Security and health care, quality education and access to higher education for all, not to speak of the retention of highly skilled jobs within the American economy.

The pioneer in analyzing what has been lost as a result of military Keynesianism was Seymour Melman (1917–2004), a professor of industrial engineering and operations research at Columbia

University. His 1970 book *Pentagon Capitalism: The Political Economy of War* was a prescient analysis of the unintended consequences of the American preoccupation with its armed forces and their weaponry since the onset of the Cold War. Melman wrote:

> From 1946 to 1969, the United States government spent over $1,000 billion on the military, more than half of this under the Kennedy and Johnson administrations—the period during which the [Pentagon-dominated] state management was established as a formal institution. This sum of staggering size (try to visualize a billion of something) does not express the cost of the military establishment to the nation as a whole. The true cost is measured by what has been foregone, by the accumulated deterioration in many facets of life by the inability to alleviate human wretchedness of long duration.

In an important exegesis on Melman's relevance to the current American economic situation, Thomas Woods has written:

> According to the U.S. Department of Defense, during the four decades from 1947 through 1987 it used (in 1982 dollars) $7.62 trillion in capital resources. In 1985, the Department of Commerce estimated the value of the nation's plant and equipment, and infrastructure, at just over $7.29 trillion. In other words, the amount spent over that period could have doubled the American capital stock or modernized and replaced its existing stock.

The fact that we did not modernize or replace our capital assets is one of the main reasons why, by the turn of the twenty-first century, our manufacturing base had all but evaporated.

Machine tools—an industry on which Melman was an authority—are a particularly important symptom. In November 1968, a five-year inventory disclosed

> that 64 percent of the metalworking machine tools used in U.S. industry were ten years old or older. The age of this industrial equipment (drills, lathes, etc.) marks the United States' machine tool stock as the oldest among all major industrial nations, and it marks the continuation of a deterioration process that began with the end of the Second World War. This deterioration at the base of the industrial system certifies to the continuous debilitating and depleting effect that the military use of capital and research and development talent has had on American industry.

Nothing has been done in the period since 1968 to reverse these trends, and it shows today in our massive imports of equipment—from medical machines such as proton accelerators for radiological therapy (made primarily in Belgium, Germany, and Japan) to cars and trucks.

Our short tenure as the world's "lone superpower" has come to an end. As Harvard economics professor Benjamin Friedman has written:

> Again and again it has always been the world's leading lending country that has been the premier country in terms of political influence, diplomatic influence, and cultural influence. It's no accident that we took over the role from the British at the same time that we took over . . . the job of being the world's leading lending country. Today we are no longer the world's leading lending country. In fact we are now the world's biggest

debtor country, and we are continuing to wield influence on the basis of military prowess alone.

Some of the damage done can never be rectified. There are, however, some steps that this country urgently needs to take. These include reversing Bush's 2001 and 2003 tax cuts for the wealthy, beginning to liquidate our global empire of more than eight hundred military bases, cutting from the defense budget all projects that bear no relationship to the national security of the United States, and ceasing to use the defense budget as a Keynesian jobs program. If we do these things we have a chance of squeaking by. If we don't, we face probable national insolvency and a long depression.

12

THE MILITARY-INDUSTRIAL MAN

September 14, 2004

It is hardly news to anyone who pays the slightest attention to American politics that Congress is no longer responsive to the people. Incumbency is so well institutionalized that elections generally mean virtually nothing.

In one district after another the weapons industry has bought the incumbent and the voters are unable to dislodge him or her. On really big projects like the B-2 stealth bomber, contracts for pieces of the airplane are placed in all of the forty-eight continental states to ensure that individual members of Congress can be threatened with the loss of jobs in their districts should they ever get the idea that we do not need another weapon of massive destruction. The result is massive defense budgets, leading to the highest governmental deficits in postwar history. It seems likely that only bankruptcy will stop the American imperial juggernaut.

The California 50th Congressional District in northern San Diego County, where I live, is a good example of exactly how this works at the local level. The constituents of the 50th District have been misrepresented in Washington for the past fourteen years by a wholly paid for tool of the military-industrial complex—the Republican incumbent, Randy "Duke" Cunningham.

The heavily populated 50th District is an oddly gerryman-dered amalgam of rich (and Republican) Rancho Santa Fe and La Jolla, more liberal coastal towns like the northern sections of San Diego itself, Del Mar, Encinitas, and Carlsbad, and—inland—Hispanic and working-class Escondido and Mira Mesa. Although the district includes much of La Jolla, it excludes the University of California campus and the students who live and work there. It's a district whose character has shifted in recent years as thou-sands of biotech researchers and other professionals have moved into the area and as parts of educated, white-collar San Diego have been included in it as well. The 50th District is desperately in need of new leadership in Congress more in tune with the political values and interests of the people who now live there. In 2004, for the first time, Cunningham is opposed by a candidate who is well qualified and whose views—if they were better known—more clearly match the interests and values of the people he claims to represent.

From July 12 through 14, Decision Research, one of the most respected polling firms in the country, conducted a telephone poll of 440 registered voters in the district. Among its findings were that when they heard Cunningham's voting record on abor-tion, school vouchers, protecting the environment, the Iraq war, spending on weapons, and many other issues, his lead dropped from 18 to 4 percentage points, within the poll's 4.7 percent margin of error. The relatively unknown Democratic candidate running against him is Francine Busby, past president of one of the district's school boards, who has nonetheless put together a powerful campaign, particularly among women, drawing attention to the way Cunningham has sold out the welfare of the district to special interests.

Sources of information on Cunningham are his and his opponents' reports to the Federal Election Commission (FEC) as well as accounts of his record compiled by the three leading nonpartisan think tanks on Congress: the Center for Responsive Politics in Washington, Political Moneyline, and Project Vote Smart in Philipsburg, Montana.

Let's start with money. As of June 30, 2004, Cunningham had raised $608,977 for the coming election, spent $382,043, and as cash on hand had an amazing $890,753. By contrast, on the same date Francine Busby had raised $64,449, spent $32,937, and had cash on hand of $31,511. Some 46 percent of Cunningham's money comes from political action committees, so-called PACs, 49 percent from individual contributions, and none from his own personal funds. Two percent of Busby's money comes from PACs, 86 percent from individuals, and 6 percent from the candidate herself. Some 68 percent of Cunningham's money originates in California, but 32 percent of it comes from out of state. Ninety-seven percent of Busby's minuscule funds come from within California and only 3 percent from out of state. She is raising money fast but Cunningham can still outspend her 8 to 1, and he has declared publicly that his is a safe district and that he will devote his time this fall to helping George W. Bush.

The real differences show up when one examines who contributes what to whom. By industrial categories, Cunningham's top contributors, based on FEC data released August 2, 2004, are defense electronics ($66,550), defense aerospace ($39,000), lobbyists ($32,500), miscellaneous defense ($29,200), air transport ($26,500), health professionals ($24,700), and real estate ($23,001). Busby's top contributors are listed as "retired." Cunningham's number one financial backer is the Titan Corporation of San Diego, which gave him $18,000. It has recently been in the news for supplying Arabic translators to the Army, several of whom have been identified as possible torturers at Abu Ghraib prison in Baghdad. Titan's $657 million Pentagon contract, which had to be approved by the House Appropriations Committee's National Security Subcommittee, of which Cunningham is a member, is the company's single biggest source of revenue, so it's a clear case of a political payoff.

Lockheed Martin, the world's largest weapons manufacturer, gave Cunningham a whopping $15,000. Cunningham's number three source of funds is MZM Inc. of Washington, D.C., whose government clients, in addition to the Pentagon, include the "U.S. intelligence community," the "Foreign Terrorist Tracking Task Force," and the Department of Homeland Security. MZM gave Randy $11,000 for his services. Next in line is the Cubic Corporation of San Diego, which has numerous multimillion-dollar contracts with the Pentagon to supply "realistic combat training systems" and surveillance and reconnaissance avionics. It gave Randy $10,000. General Dynamics ponied up $10,000 for the congressman, as did San Diego's Science Applications International Corporation, or SAIC as it is commonly known. SAIC's largest customer by far is the U.S. government, which accounts for 69 percent of its business according to SAIC's filings with the SEC. (SAIC was supposed to build a new, pro-American TV and radio network in Iraq but bungled the job badly.) The remainder of Cunningham's top contributors reads like a Who's Who among the merchants of death: $9,500 from Northrop Grumman, $8,000 from Raytheon (which makes the Tomahawk cruise missile), $8,500 from Qualcomm, and $7,000 from Boeing. All this for just one congressman.

Busby's biggest contributions are $2,000 from an outfit called

"Blue Hornet," which designs websites, $1,835 from members of the Cardiff School Board, and $1,080 from employees of Mira Costa College.

One ingenious measure of how money displaces people in our political system, compiled by the Center for Responsive Politics, is the zip codes from which each candidate gets his or her individual contributions. For Cunningham the chief one is 92067, Rancho Santa Fe, with $62,795 in donations. Rancho Santa Fe is well known as a beautiful, underpopulated enclave of extremely wealthy people, many of them foreigners. It is followed by 92037, La Jolla, not a poor town, which chipped in $24,000 for Cunningham. The next two zip codes are 20003 and 20007, both of which are in Washington, D.C. Cunningham received the fewest donations from 92065, Carlsbad. Busby's are the direct opposite. Her best zip code is 92007, her hometown of Cardiff, the residents of which have given her $8,415, followed by 92009, Carlsbad; 92014, Del Mar; and last 92091, wealthy Fairbanks Ranch, which gave her a mere $1,000. Cunningham's money comes from the following localities, in descending order: San Diego, Washington, D.C., New York City, and Orange County, California. Busby's comes entirely from the San Diego metropolitan area.

Cunningham knows with precision who gives him money and what its providers expect of him. As the Japanese like to say, you don't have to tell a geisha what to do. He has 100 percent ratings from the National Right to Life Committee (he is adamantly opposed to giving women the right to choose), the League of Private Property Voters, the Christian Coalition, and the Business-Industry PAC, and an 80 percent rating from the Gun Owners of America. Over the last decade he has received $44,600 from the National Rifle Association, more than any other member of Congress except Representative Don Young, a Republican from

Alaska. There are no places in the 50th District to go hunting, least of all with an Uzi or an AK-47.

Cunningham's voting record likewise reflects the fact that national neoconservatives and the munitions industry now own him lock, stock, and barrel. As one might expect, he voted for the No Child Left Behind and PATRIOT acts. He also voted yes on the following measures: the law banning partial birth abortion; the $350 billion tax break for the rich, passed on May 23, 2003, by a vote of 231 to 200; a law prohibiting liability lawsuits against gun makers and gun sellers whose products are used to commit crimes; the Medicare Prescription Drug Act, passed in the middle of the night on November 22, 2003, by a vote of 220 to 215; and the Emergency Wartime Supplemental Appropriations Act of April 3, 2003, that included $62.5 billion for the war in Iraq.

Cunningham talks a lot about patriotism and putting the country first, but although his voting record in 2003 was 98 percent for what President Bush wanted, in 1999 he had only a 20 percent record of supporting President Clinton. Opposition to Clinton is, of course, almost the functional definition of "patriotism" among Cunningham's wing of the Republican Party, which sought to impeach the president for a venial sin but which is indifferent to evidence of mortal sins committed by President Bush, particularly his leading the country into war against Iraq based on a tissue of lies.

Within Congress, Cunningham is a member of the National Security Subcommittee of the Appropriations Committee, a forum the military-industrial complex does everything in its power to control, and of the Permanent Select Committee on Intelligence. The latter is the committee headed by Congressman Porter Goss of Florida, a former CIA agent nominated by President Bush to be the next director of the CIA. This oversight committee has not exactly covered itself with glory, approving the work of the CIA even as it was failing to warn the country about the attacks of 9/11 and deceiving Congress and the people into war with Iraq.

According to Cunningham himself, his most important lifetime achievement is his twenty years of service as a naval aviator, including aerial combat over Vietnam in which he shot down three communist jets in one day (overall, a total of five during the war) and was himself brought down by a surface-to-air missile. On May 10, 1972, he was rescued by a helicopter from the South China Sea. Cunningham has exploited this record into what one commentator calls "hero inflation" and Shakespeare's Henry V called "remembering with advantages." He now claims to have been a military hero deserving of the Congressional Medal of Honor (which he didn't get), even though he acknowledges that his aerial dogfighting had little effect on the course of the war. Cunningham has created a company called Top Gun Enterprises that sells lithographs of himself in his pilot's outfit and books he has written about his Navy exploits. His company's website claims that the 1986 film *Top Gun* starring Tom Cruise was actually about Randy "Duke" Cunningham.

Cunningham's comments in the *Congressional Record* dwell heavily on his Vietnam role and the military. For example, on April 22, 2004, he said to the House of Representatives: "Mr. Speaker, I was shot down over North Vietnam. I can remember the anger and the disparaging remarks that John Kerry made about our service. I remember the rage in all of us from his slander. . . . Even today, John Kerry votes against defense, the military, veterans, and intelligence bills that would enforce the safe return of our men and women. We do not need someone that would vote like a Jane Fonda as commander in chief."

He persisted in such attacks on the patriotism of Kerry,

notably in an interview with Rush Limbaugh on August 17, 2004. Here's an excerpt:

DUKE: It's not about Vietnam. It's about what he did in 1971, bad-mouthing all of us, calling us war criminals. It's his votes since he's been in the Senate, he ran on cutting defense and intel, after the first Trade Center bombing, he tried to cut intelligence $9 billion. And it's about who is going to protect my family, my daughters, my son, my wife in the next few years, and to me, it's not Senator Kerry. Rush, if Senator Kerry was a Republican running, I would oppose him.

RUSH: Congressman, thanks very much for the call. It really is an honor to hear from you. I know your history and I've been very impressed with it, and you're one of the guys still taking a lot of shots because of who you are in Washington. You stand up to 'em and we all appreciate it, we honor your service here. Thanks very much.

DUKE: Life is good, Rush.

RUSH: It is. That's Duke Cunningham, congressman from California, the first fighter ace in Vietnam, five MiGs shot down.

Cunningham's most famous naval exploit actually occurred after he left the Navy and was a freshman congressman. In 1991, Cunningham was a member of the board of directors of the Tailhook Association, a private group of active duty, reserve, and retired Navy and Marine Corps aviators, defense contractors, and their supporters. (The name "Tailhook" comes from the device that halts aircraft when they land on aircraft carriers.) The Navy used to provide free office space for the association at San Diego's Miramar Naval Air Station, and lent out its fleet of passenger aircraft to fly attendees to Tailhook's yearly meetings in Las

Vegas. At the 35th Annual Tailhook Symposium (September 5–7, 1991) at the Las Vegas Hilton, a meeting that Cunningham attended in an official capacity, drunken fliers, joined by the secretary of the Navy, groped, stripped, and mauled some eighty-three women in the hotel, according to the report of the Department of Defense's Inspector General.

Since that time, Cunningham has devoted massive amounts of time and energy to arguing that what went on was just good clean fun and great male bonding. In congressional hearings, he has gone out of his way to undercut official programs to combat sexual harassment and discrimination in the military. According to the *San Diego Union-Tribune* of March 11, 1998, he referred to such efforts as "B.S." and "political correctness." In 1998, after Cunningham had been operated on for prostate cancer, he commented to the press, "The only person who would enjoy a prostate biopsy is Barney Frank." His fellow congressman Barney Frank (D-MA), who is openly gay, replied, "Cunningham seems to be more obsessed with homosexuality than most homosexuals."

Cunningham has only one string to his mandolin: the military-industrial complex and its interests. He has virtually no record at all on such issues as illegal immigration, water resources, ocean pollution, agriculture, mass transit, renewable energy, and unemployment. Whenever he takes up subjects such as environmental conservation and education, it is to reduce or halt federal funds that might make a difference. Citizens of the 50th District are not uninterested in national security, but they have a much broader range of needs and concerns than has ever crossed the mind of their current representative. As one of Cunningham's constituents, I hope we send to the House of Representatives a person who actually knows something about the communities of northern San Diego County. A Francine Busby victory this November would cause a political realignment in San Diego County comparable to Loretta Sanchez's 1996 defeat of "B-1" Bob Dornan in Orange County's 46th District.*

---

* In November 2004, Cunningham soundly defeated Busby with 59 percent of the vote to her 37 percent, but what voters did not do, his own greed did. In 2005, the Republican resigned from Congress after pleading guilty to taking $2.4 million in bribes from defense contractors. This "unparalleled corruption," in the words of federal prosecutors, included his use of a "bribe menu" on congressional letterhead that spelled out the kickbacks required for him to steer contracts to various businesses. In 2006, Cunningham was sentenced to more than eight years in prison for bribery and tax evasion. That June, Republican Brian Bilbray, a former congressman, defeated Busby in a contentious special election race for Cunningham's seat. In a November rematch, Bilbray bested Busby a second time. In early 2007, Carole Lam, the U.S. attorney in San Diego who prosecuted Cunningham, was forced to resign by the Bush administration. The system of "earmarks" used by Cunningham and others in Congress to fund favorite projects and the powerful lobbying efforts of the military-industrial complex remain in place.

13

WE HAVE THE MONEY

(IF ONLY WE DIDN'T WASTE IT ON THE DEFENSE BUDGET)

September 28, 2008

There has been much moaning, air sucking, and outrage about the $700 billion that the U.S. government is thinking of throwing away on rich New York bankers who have been ripping us off for the past few years and then letting greed drive their businesses into a variety of ditches. In fact, we dole out similar amounts of money every year in the form of payoffs to the armed services, the military-industrial complex, and powerful senators and representatives allied with the Pentagon.

On Wednesday, September 24, right in the middle of the fight over billions of taxpayer dollars slated to bail out Wall Street, the House of Representatives passed a $612 billion defense authorization bill for 2009 without a murmur of public protest or any meaningful press comment at all. (The *New York Times* gave the matter only three short paragraphs buried in a story about another appropriations measure.)

The defense bill includes $68.6 billion to pursue the wars in Iraq and Afghanistan, which is only a down payment on the full yearly cost of these wars. (The rest will be raised through future supplementary bills.) It also included a 3.9 percent pay raise for military personnel, and $5 billion in pork-barrel projects not even requested by the administration or the secretary of defense. It also fully funds the Pentagon's request for a radar site in the Czech Republic, a harebrained scheme sure to infuriate the Russians just as much as a Russian missile base in Cuba once infuriated us. The whole bill passed by a vote of 392–39 and will fly through the Senate, where a similar bill has already been approved. And no one will even think to mention it in the same breath with the discussion of bailout funds for dying investment banks and the like.

This is pure waste. Our annual spending on "national security"—meaning the defense budget plus all military expenditures hidden in the budgets for the departments of Energy, State, Treasury, Veterans Affairs, the CIA, and numerous other places in the executive branch—already exceeds a trillion dollars, an amount larger than that of all other national defense budgets combined. Not only was there no significant media coverage of this latest appropriation, there have been no signs of even the slightest urge to inquire into the relationship between our bloated military, our staggering weapons expenditures, our extravagantly expensive failed wars abroad, and the financial catastrophe on Wall Street.

The only congressional "commentary" on the size of our military outlay was the usual pompous drivel about how a failure to vote for the defense authorization bill would betray our troops. The aged Senator John Warner (R-VA), former chairman of the Senate Armed Services Committee, implored his Republican colleagues to vote for the bill "out of respect for military personnel." He seems to be unaware that these troops are actually volunteers, not draftees, and that they joined the armed forces as a matter of career choice rather than because the nation demanded such a sacrifice from them.

We would better respect our armed forces by bringing the

futile and misbegotten wars in Iraq and Afghanistan to an end. A relative degree of peace and order has returned to Iraq not because of President Bush's belated reinforcement of our expeditionary army there (the so-called surge), but thanks to shifting internal dynamics within Iraq and in the Middle East region generally. Such shifts include a growing awareness among Iraq's Sunni population of the need to restore law and order, a growing confidence among Iraqi Shiites of their nearly unassailable position of political influence in the country, and a growing awareness among Sunni nations that the ill-informed war of aggression the Bush administration waged against Iraq has vastly increased the influence of Shiism and Iran in the region.

The continued presence of American troops and their heavily reinforced bases in Iraq threaten this return to relative stability. The refusal of the Shia government of Iraq to agree to an American Status of Forces Agreement that would exempt off-duty American troops from Iraqi law—much desired by the Bush administration—is actually a good sign for the future of Iraq.

In Afghanistan, our historically deaf generals and civilian strategists do not seem to understand that our defeat by the Afghan insurgents is inevitable. Since the time of Alexander the Great, no foreign intruder has ever prevailed over Afghan guerrillas defending their home turf. The first Anglo-Afghan War (1838–42) marked a particularly humiliating defeat of British imperialism at the very height of English military power in the Victorian era. The Soviet-Afghan War (1979–89) resulted in a Russian defeat so demoralizing that it contributed significantly to the disintegration of the former Soviet Union in 1991. We are now on track to repeat virtually all the errors committed by previous invaders of Afghanistan over the centuries.

In the past year, perhaps most disastrously, we have carried our Afghan war into Pakistan, a relatively wealthy and sophisticated nuclear power that has long cooperated with us militarily. Our bungling brutality along the Afghan-Pakistan border threatens to radicalize the Pashtuns in both countries and advance the interests of radical Islam throughout the region. The United States is now identified in each country mainly with Hellfire missiles, unmanned drones, special operations raids, and repeated incidents of the killing of innocent bystanders.

The brutal bombing of the Marriott Hotel in Pakistan's capital, Islamabad, on September 20, 2008, was a powerful indicator of the spreading strength of virulent anti-American sentiment in the area. The hotel was a well-known watering hole for American Marines, Special Forces troops, and CIA agents. Our military activities in Pakistan have been as misguided as the Nixon-Kissinger invasion of Cambodia in 1970. The end result will almost surely be the same.

We should begin our disengagement from Afghanistan at once. We dislike the Taliban's fundamentalist religious values, but the Afghan public, with its desperate desire for a return of law and order and the curbing of corruption, knows that the Taliban is the only political force in the country that has ever brought the opium trade under control. The Pakistanis and their effective army can defend their country from Taliban domination so long as we abandon the activities that are causing both Afghans and Pakistanis to see the Taliban as a lesser evil.

One of America's greatest authorities on the defense budget, Winslow Wheeler, worked for thirty-one years for Republican members of the Senate and for the General Accounting Office on military expenditures. His conclusion, when it comes to the fiscal sanity of our military spending, is devastating.

America's defense budget is now larger in inflation-adjusted dollars than at any point since the end of World War II, and yet our Army has fewer combat brigades than at any point in that period; our Navy has fewer combat ships; and the Air Force has fewer combat aircraft. Our major equipment inventories for these major forces are older on average than any point since 1946—or in some cases, in our entire history.

This in itself is a national disgrace. Spending hundreds of billions of dollars on present and future wars that have nothing to do with our national security is simply obscene. And yet Congress has been corrupted by the military-industrial complex into believing that by voting for more defense spending, they are supplying "jobs" for the economy. In fact, they are only diverting scarce resources from the desperately needed rebuilding of the American infrastructure and other crucial spending necessities into utterly wasteful munitions. If we cannot cut back our long-standing, ever increasing military spending in a major way, then the bankruptcy of the United States is inevitable. As the current Wall Street meltdown has demonstrated, that is no longer an abstract possibility but a growing likelihood. We do not have much time left.

14

ECONOMIC DEATH SPIRAL
AT THE PENTAGON

February 2, 2009

Like much of the rest of the world, Americans know that the U.S. automotive industry is in the grip of what may be a fatal decline. Unless it receives emergency financing *and* undergoes significant reform, it is undoubtedly headed for the graveyard in which many American industries are already buried, including those that made televisions and other consumer electronics, many types of scientific and medical equipment, machine tools, textiles, and much earth-moving equipment—and that's to name only the most obvious candidates. They all lost their competitiveness to newly emerging economies that were able to outpace them in innovative design, price, quality, service, and fuel economy, among other things.

A similar, if far less well known, crisis exists when it comes to the military-industrial complex. That crisis has its roots in the corrupt and deceitful practices that have long characterized the high command of the armed forces, civilian executives of the armaments industries, and congressional opportunists and criminals looking for pork-barrel projects, defense installations for their districts, or even bribes for votes.

Given our economic crisis, the estimated trillion dollars we spend each year on the military and its weaponry is simply unsustainable. Even if present fiscal constraints no longer existed, we would still have misspent too much of our tax revenues on too few, overly expensive, overly complex weapons systems that leave us ill prepared to defend the country in a real military emergency. We face a double crisis at the Pentagon: we can no longer afford the pretense of being the earth's sole superpower, and we cannot afford to perpetuate a system in which the military-industrial complex makes its fortune off inferior, poorly designed weapons.

DOUBLE CRISIS AT THE PENTAGON

This self-destructive system of bloated budgets and purchases of the wrong weapons has persisted for so long thanks to the aura of invincibility surrounding the armed forces and a mistaken belief that jobs in the arms industry are as valuable to the economy as jobs in the civilian sector.

Chairman of the Joint Chiefs of Staff Admiral Michael Mullen has advocated nothing less than protecting the Pentagon budget by pegging defense spending to a fixed percentage of gross domestic product (GDP, the total value of goods and services produced by the economy). This would, of course, mean simply throwing out serious strategic analysis of what is actually needed for national defense. Mullen wants, instead, to raise the annual defense budget in the worst of times to at least 4 percent of GDP. Such a policy is clearly designed to deceive the public about the ludicrously wasteful spending on weapons systems that has gone on for decades.

It is hard to imagine any sector of the American economy more driven by ideology, delusion, and propaganda than the armed services. Many people believe that our military is the largest, best equipped, and most invincible among the world's armed forces. None of these things is true, but our military is, without a doubt, the most expensive to maintain. Each year, we Americans account for nearly half of all global military spending, an amount larger than the next forty-five nations together spend on their militaries annually.

Equally striking, the military seems increasingly ill adapted to the types of wars that Pentagon strategists agree the United States is most likely to fight in the future, and that it is in fact already fighting in Afghanistan—insurgencies led by nonstate actors. While the Department of Defense produces weaponry meant for such wars, it is also squandering staggering levels of defense appropriations on aircraft, ships, and futuristic weapons systems that fascinate generals and admirals and that are beloved by military contractors mainly because their complexity runs up their cost to astronomical levels.

That most of these will actually prove irrelevant to the world in which we live matters not a whit to their makers or purchasers. Thought of another way, the stressed-out American taxpayer, already supporting two disastrous wars and the weapons systems that go with them, is also paying good money for weapons that are meant for fantasy wars, for wars that will only be fought in the battlescapes and war-gaming imaginations of Defense Department "planners."

The Air Force and the Army are still planning as if, in the reasonably near future, they were going to fight an old-fashioned war of attrition against the Soviet Union, which disappeared in 1991, while the Navy, with its eleven large aircraft-carrier battle groups, is, as William S. Lind has written, "still structured to fight the Imperial Japanese Navy." Lind, a prominent theorist of so-called fourth-generation warfare (insurgencies carried out by groups such as al-Qaeda), argues that "the Navy's aircraft-carrier battle groups have cruised on mindlessly for more than half a century, waiting for those Japanese carriers to turn up. They are still cruising today, into, if not beyond, irrelevance. . . . Submarines are today's and tomorrow's capital ships; the ships that most directly determine control of blue waters."

In December 2008, Franklin "Chuck" Spinney, a former high-ranking civilian in the Pentagon's Office of Systems Analysis (set up in 1961 to make independent evaluations of Pentagon policy) and a charter member of the "Fighter Mafia" of the 1980s and 1990s, wrote, "As has been documented for at least twenty years, patterns of repetitive habitual behavior in the Pentagon have created a self-destructive decision-making process. This process has produced a death spiral."

As a result, concluded Spinney, inadequate amounts of wildly overpriced equipment are purchased, "new weapons [that] do not replace old ones on a one for one basis." There is also "continual pressure to reduce combat readiness," a "corrupt accounting system" that "makes it impossible to sort out the priorities," and a readiness to believe that old solutions will work for the current crisis.

FAILED REFORM EFFORTS

There's no great mystery about the causes of the deep dysfunction that has long characterized the Pentagon's weapons procurement system. In 2006, Thomas Christie, former head of Operational Test and Evaluation, the most senior official at the Department of Defense for testing weapons and a Pentagon veteran of half a century, detailed more than thirty-five years of efforts to reform the weapons acquisition system. These included the 1971 Fitzhugh (or Blue Ribbon) Commission, the 1977 Steadman Review, the 1981 Carlucci Acquisition Initiatives, the 1986 Packard Commission, the 1986 Goldwater-Nichols Department of Defense Reorganization Act, the 1989 Defense Management Review, the 1990 "Streamlining Review" of the Defense Science Board, the 1993–94 report of the Acquisition Streamlining Task Force and of the Defense Science Board, the late 1990s Total System Performance Responsibility initiative of the Air Force, and the Capabilities-Based Acquisition approach of the Missile Defense Agency of the first years of this century.

Christie concluded: "After all these years of repeated reform efforts, major defense programs are taking 20 to 30 years to deliver less capability than planned, very often at two to three times the costs and schedules planned." He also added the following observations:

> Launching into major developments without understanding key technical issues is the root cause of major cost and schedule problems. . . . Costs, schedules, and technical risks are often grossly understated at the outset. . . . There are more acquisition programs being pursued than DoD [the Department of Defense] can possibly afford in the long term. . . .
>
> By the time these problems are acknowledged, the political penalties incurred in enforcing any major restructuring of a program, much less its cancellation, are too painful to bear. Unless someone is willing to stand up and point out that the emperor has no clothes, the U.S. military will continue to hemorrhage taxpayer dollars and critical years while acquiring equipment that falls short of meeting the needs of troops in the field.

The inevitable day of reckoning long predicted by Pentagon critics has, I believe, finally arrived. Our problems are those of a very rich country that has become accustomed over the years to defense budgets that are actually jobs programs and also a major source of pork for the use of politicians in their reelection campaigns.

Given the present major recession, whose depths remain unknown, the United States has better things to spend its money on than Nimitz-class aircraft carriers at a price of $6.2 billion each (the cost of the USS *George H. W. Bush*, launched in January 2009), or aircraft that can cruise at a speed of Mach 2 (1,352 miles per hour).

However, don't wait for the Pentagon to sort out such matters. If it has proven one thing over the last decades, it's that it is thoroughly incapable of reforming itself. According to Christie, "Over the past 20 or so years, the DoD and its components have deliberately and systematically decimated their in-house technical capabilities to the point where there is little, if any, competence or initiative left in the various organizations tasked with planning and executing its budget and acquisition programs."

GUNNING FOR THE AIR FORCE

President Obama almost certainly retained Robert M. Gates as secretary of defense in part to give himself some bipartisan cover as he tries to come to grips with the bloated defense budget. Gates was also sympathetic to the desire of a few reformers in the Pentagon to dump the Lockheed-Martin F-22 Raptor supersonic stealth fighter, a plane designed to meet the Soviet Union's last proposed, but never built, interceptor.

The Air Force's old guard and its allies in Congress fought back aggressively. In June 2008, Gates fired Secretary of the Air

Force Michael W. Wynne and Air Force Chief of Staff General T. Michael Moseley. Though he was undoubtedly responding to their fervent support for the F-22, his cover explanation was their visible failure to adequately supervise the accounting and control of nuclear weapons.

In 2006, the Air Force had managed to ship to Taiwan four high-tech nose cone fuses for Minuteman ICBM warheads instead of promised helicopter batteries, an error that went blissfully undetected until March 2008. Then, in August 2007, a B-52 bomber carrying six *armed* nuclear cruise missiles flew across much of the country, from Minot Air Force Base in North Dakota to Barksdale Air Force Base in Louisiana. This was in direct violation of standing orders against such flights over the United States.

As Julian Barnes and Peter Spiegel of the *Los Angeles Times* noted in June 2008, "Tensions between the Air Force and Gates have been growing for months," mainly over Gates's frustration about the F-22 and his inability to get the Air Force to deploy more pilotless aircraft to the various war zones. They were certainly not improved when Wynne, a former senior vice president of General Dynamics, went out of his way to cross Gates, arguing publicly that "any president would be damn happy to have more F-22s around if we had to get into a fight with China." It catches something of the power of the military-industrial complex that despite his clear desire on the subject, Gates has been slow to move when it comes to pulling the plug on the F-22; nor has he even dared to bring up the subject of canceling its more expensive and technically complicated successor, the F-35 "Joint Strike Fighter."*

---

* After a bruising lobbying battle in the Senate, the Obama administration was able to kill the F-22 program in July 2009. Lockheed, however, hardly lost out. A month later, Defense Secretary Robert Gates announced his support for the F-35 and even pressed for a production ramp-up for that plane, while publicly emphasizing the need to keep the program on budget and on schedule. Plans were then announced for the purchase of 513 F-35s through 2015 and, ultimately, a fleet of 2,443 planes.

More than twenty years ago, Chuck Spinney wrote a classic account of the now routine bureaucratic scams practiced within the Pentagon to ensure that Congress will appropriate funds for dishonestly advertised and promoted weapons systems and then prevent their cancellation when the fraud comes to light. In a paper he entitled "Defense Power Games," of which his superiors deeply disapproved, Spinney outlined two crucial Pentagon gambits meant to lock in such weaponry: "front-loading" and "political engineering."

It should be understood at the outset that all actors involved, including the military officers in charge of projects, the members of Congress who use defense appropriations to buy votes within their districts, and the contractors who live off the ensuing lucrative contracts, utilize these two scams. It is also important to understand that neither front-loading nor political engineering is an innocent or morally neutral maneuver. They both involve criminal intent to turn on the spigot of taxpayer money and then to jam it so that it cannot be turned off. They are de rigueur practices of our military-industrial complex.

Front-loading is the practice of appropriating funds for a new weapons project based solely on assurances by its official sponsors about what it can do. This happens long before a prototype has been built or tested, and it invariably involves the quoting of unrealistically low unit costs for a sizable order. Assurances are always given that the system's technical requirements will be simple or have already been met. Lowballing future costs, an intrinsic aspect of front-loading, is an old Defense Department

---

In November, word emerged that the program was already behind schedule and over budget. As a result, in January 2010, the Pentagon proposed delays and production cuts for the F-35. Lockheed, however, would still not lose out, since such delays would only curtail the program in the short term, while the total number of planes purchased would ultimately remain unchanged.

trick, a governmental version of bait-and-switch. What is introduced as a great bargain regularly turns out to be a grossly expensive lemon.

Political engineering is the strategy of awarding contracts in as many different congressional districts as possible. By making voters and congressional incumbents dependent on military money, the Pentagon's political engineers put pressure on them to continue supporting front-loaded programs even after their true costs become apparent.

Front-loading and political engineering generate several typical features in the weapons that the Pentagon then buys for its arsenal. These continually prove unnecessarily expensive, are prone to break down easily, and are often unworkably complex. They tend to come with inadequate supplies of spare parts and ammunition, since there is not enough money to buy the quantities that are needed. They also force the services to repair older weapons and keep them in service much longer than is normal or wise. For example, the B-52 bomber, which went into service in 1955, is still on active duty.

Even though extended training would seem to be a necessary corollary to the complexity of such weapons systems, the excessive cost actually leads to reductions in training time for pilots and others. In the long run, it is because of such expedients and short-term fixes that American casualties may increase and, sooner or later, battles or wars may be lost.

For example, Northrop Grumman's much touted B-2 stealth bomber has proven to be almost totally worthless. It is too delicate to deploy to harsh climates without special hangars first being built to protect it at ridiculous expense; it cannot fulfill any combat missions that older designs were not fully adequate to perform; and—at a total cost of $44.75 billion for only twenty-one bombers—it wastes resources needed for real combat situations.

Instead, in military terms, the most unexpectedly successful post-Vietnam aircraft has been the Fairchild A-10, unflatteringly nicknamed the "Warthog." It is the only close-support aircraft ever developed by the U.S. Air Force. Its task is to loiter over battlefields and assist ground forces in disposing of obstinate or formidable targets, which is not something that fits comfortably with the Air Force's hotshot self-image.

Some 715 A-10s were produced, and they served with great effectiveness in the first Persian Gulf War. All 715 cumulatively cost less than three B-2 bombers. The A-10 is now out of production because the Air Force establishment favors extremely fast aircraft that fly in straight lines at high altitudes rather than aircraft that are useful in battle. In the Afghan war, the Air Force has regularly inflicted heavy casualties on innocent civilians at least in part because it tries to attack ground targets from the air with inappropriately high-performance equipment.

USING THE F-22 TO FIGHT THE F-16

The military-industrial complex is today so confident of its skills in gaming the system that it does not hesitate to publicize how many workers in a particular district will lose their jobs if a particular project is canceled. Threats are also made—and put into effect—to withhold political contributions from uncooperative congressional representatives.

As Spinney recalls, "In July 1989, when some members of Congress began to build a coalition aimed at canceling the B-2, Northrop Corporation, the B-2's prime contractor, retaliated by releasing data which had previously been classified showing that tens of thousands of jobs and hundreds of millions in profits were at risk in 46 states and 383 congressional districts." The B-2 was not canceled.

Southern California's biggest private employers are Boeing Corporation and Northrop Grumman. They are said to employ more than 58,000 workers in well-paying jobs, a major political obstacle to rationalizing defense expenditures even as recession is making such steps all but unavoidable.

Both front-loading and political engineering are alive and well. They are in fact now at the center of fierce controversies surrounding the extreme age of the present fleet of Air Force fighter aircraft, most of which date from the 1980s. Meanwhile, the costs of the two most likely successors to the workhorse F-16—the F-22 Raptor and the F-35 Joint Strike Fighter—have run up so high that the government cannot afford to purchase significant numbers of either of them.

The F-16 made its first flight in December 1976, and a total of 4,400 have been built. They have been sold, or given away, all over the world. Planning for the F-22 began in 1986, when the Cold War was still alive (even if on life support), and the Air Force was trumpeting its fears that the other superpower, the USSR, was planning a new, ultrafast, highly maneuverable fighter.

By the time the prototype F-22 had its rollout on May 11, 1997, the Cold War was nearly a decade in its grave, and it was perfectly apparent that the Soviet aircraft it was intended to match would never be built. Lockheed Martin, the F-22's prime contractor, naturally argued that we needed it anyway and made plans to sell some 438 airplanes for a total tab of $70 billion. By mid-2008, only 183 F-22s were on order, 122 of which had been delivered. The numbers had been reduced due to cost overruns. The Air Force still wanted to buy an additional 198 planes, but Secretary Gates and his leading assistants balked. No wonder. According to arms experts Bill Hartung and Christopher Preble, at more than $350 million each, the F-22 is "the most expensive fighter plane ever built."

The F-22 has several strikingly expensive characteristics, which actually limit its usefulness. It is allegedly a stealth fighter—that is, an airplane with a shape that reduces its visibility on radar—but there is no such thing as an airplane completely invisible to all radar. In any case, once it turns on its own fire-control radar, which it must do in combat, it becomes fully visible to an enemy.

The F-22 is able to maneuver at very high altitudes, but this is of limited value since there are no other airplanes in service anywhere that can engage in combat at such heights. It can cruise at twice the speed of sound in level flight without the use of its afterburners (which consume fuel at an accelerated rate), but there are no potential adversaries for which these capabilities are relevant. The plane is obviously blindingly irrelevant to "fourth-generation wars" such as that with the Taliban in Afghanistan—the sorts of conflicts for which American strategists inside the Pentagon and out believe the United States should be preparing.

Actually, the United States ought not to be engaged in fourth-generation wars at all, whatever planes are in its fleet. Outside powers normally find such wars unwinnable. Unfortunately, President Obama's approach to the Bush administration's Afghan war remains deeply flawed and will only entrap us in another quagmire, whatever planes we put in the skies over that country.

Nonetheless, as he entered office, the F-22 was still being promoted as the plane to buy, almost entirely through front-loading and political engineering. Some apologists for the Air Force also claimed that we needed the F-22 to face the F-16. Their argument went this way: We have sold so many F-16s to allies and Third World customers that if we ever had to fight one of them, that country might prevail using our own equipment against us. Some foreign air forces like Israel's are fully equipped with F-16s, and their pilots actually receive more training and monthly practice hours than ours do.

This, however, seems a trivial reason for funding more F-22s. We should instead simply not get involved in wars with former allies we have armed, although this is why Congress prohibited Lockheed from selling the F-22 abroad. Some Pentagon critics contend that the Air Force and prime contractors lobby for arms sales abroad because they artificially generate a demand for new weapons at home that are "better" than the ones we've sold elsewhere.

Thanks to political engineering, the F-22 has parts suppliers in forty-four states, and some 25,000 people have well-paying jobs building it. Lockheed Martin and some in the Defense Department have therefore proposed that if the F-22 is canceled, it should be replaced by the F-35 Joint Strike Fighter, also built by Lockheed Martin.

Most serious observers believe that this would only make a bad situation worse. So far the F-35 shows every sign of being, in Chuck Spinney's words, "a far more costly and more troubled turkey" than the F-22, "even though it has a distinction that even the F-22 cannot claim, namely, it is tailored to meet the same threat that . . . ceased to exist at least three years before the F-35 R&D [research and development] program began in 1994."

The F-35 is considerably more complex than the F-22, meaning that it will undoubtedly be even more expensive to repair and will break down even more easily. Its cost per plane is guaranteed to continue to spiral upward. The design of the F-22 involves 4 million lines of computer code; the F-35, 19 million lines. The Pentagon sold the F-35 to Congress in 1998 with the promise of a unit cost of $184 million per aircraft. By 2008, that had risen to $355 million per aircraft, and the plane was already two years behind schedule.

According to Pierre M. Sprey, one of the original sponsors of the F-16, and Winslow T. Wheeler, a thirty-one-year veteran staff official on Senate defense committees, the F-35 is overweight, underpowered, and "less maneuverable than the appallingly vulnerable F-105 'lead sled' that got wiped out over North Vietnam in the Indochina War." Its makers claim that it will be a bomber as well as a fighter, but it will have a payload of only two 2,000-pound bombs, far less than American fighters of the Vietnam era. Although the Air Force praises its stealth features, it will lose these as soon as it mounts bombs under its wings, which will alter its shape most unstealthily.

It is a nonstarter for close-air-support missions because it is too fast for a pilot to be able to spot tactical targets. It is too delicate and potentially flammable to be able to withstand ground fire. If built, it will end up as the most expensive defense contract in history without offering a serious replacement for any of the fighters or fighter-bombers currently in service.

THE FIGHTER MAFIA

Every branch of the American armed forces suffers from similar "defense power games." For example, the new Virginia-class fast-attack submarines are expensive and not needed. As the *New York Times* wrote editorially, "The program is little more than a public works project to keep the Newport News, Va., and Groton, Conn., naval shipyards in business."

I have, however, concentrated on the Air Force because the collapse of internal controls over acquisitions is most obvious, as well as farthest advanced, there—and because the Air Force has for years been the branch of the armed services most deeply implicated in the ongoing debate over weapons procurement. Interestingly enough, on April 21, 2008, in one of the few optimistic developments in Pentagon politics in recent times, Secretary of Defense Gates launched a blistering attack on bureaucratism in a speech to officers at the Air War College at Maxwell Air Force Base, Alabama. In it, he singled out for praise and emulation an Air Force officer who had inspired many of that service's innovators over the past couple of generations while being truly despised by an establishment and an old guard who viewed him as an open threat to careerism.

Colonel John Boyd (1927–1997) was a significant military strategist, an exceptionally talented fighter pilot in both the Korean and Vietnam war eras, and for six years the chief instructor at the Fighter Weapons School at Nellis Air Force Base in Las Vegas. "Forty-Second Boyd" became a legend in the Air Force because of his standing claim that he could defeat any pilot, foreign or domestic, in simulated air-to-air combat within forty seconds, a bet he never lost even though he was continuously challenged.

Last April, Gates said, in part:

As this new era continues to unfold before us, the challenge I pose to you today is to become a forward-thinking officer who helps the Air Force adapt to a constantly changing strategic environment characterized by persistent conflict.

Let me illustrate by using a historical exemplar: the late Air Force Colonel John Boyd. As a thirty-year-old captain, he rewrote the manual for air-to-air combat. Boyd and the reformers he inspired would later go on to design and advocate for the F-16 and the A-10. After retiring, he would develop the principles of maneuver warfare that were credited by a former Marine Corps commandant [General Charles C. Krulak] and a secretary of defense [Dick Cheney] for the lightning victory of the first Gulf War. . . .

In accomplishing all these things, Boyd—a brilliant, eccentric, and stubborn character—had to overcome a large measure of bureaucratic resistance and institutional hostility. He had some advice that he used to pass on to his colleagues and subordinates that is worth sharing with you. Boyd would say, and I quote: "One day you will take a fork in the road, and you're going to have to make a decision about which direction you want to go. If you go one way, you can be somebody. You will have to make compromises and you will have to turn your back on your friends. But you will be a member of the club and you will get promoted and get good assignments. Or you can go the other way and you can do something—something for your country and for your Air Force and for yourself. If you decide to do something, you may not get promoted and get good assignments and you certainly will not be a favorite of your superiors. But you won't have to compromise yourself. To be somebody or to do something. In life there is often a roll call. That's when you have to make a decision. To be or to do." . . . We must heed John Boyd's advice by asking if the ways we do business make sense.

Boyd's many accomplishments are documented in Robert Coram's excellent biography *Boyd: The Fighter Pilot Who Changed the Art of War.* They need not be retold here. It was, however, the spirit of Boyd and "the reformers he inspired," a group within Air Force headquarters who came to be called the "Fighter Mafia," that launched the defense reform movement of the 1980s and 1990s. Their objectives were to stop the acquisition of unnecessarily complex and expensive weapons, cause the Air Force to take seriously the idea of a fourth generation of warfare, end its reliance on a strategy of attrition, and expose to criticism an officers' corps focused on careerist standards.

Unless Secretary Gates succeeds in reviving it, their lingering influence in the Pentagon is just about exhausted today. Despite Gates's praise of Boyd, one should not underestimate the formidable obstacles to Pentagon reform. Over a quarter century ago, back in 1982, journalist James Fallows outlined the most serious structural obstacle to any genuine reform in his National Book Award–winning study, *National Defense*. The book was so influential that at least one commentator includes Fallows as a non-Pentagon member of Boyd's "Fighter Mafia."

As Fallows then observed:

> The culture of procurement teaches officers that there are two paths to personal survival. One is to bring home the bacon for the service as the manager of a program that gets its full funding. "Procurement management is more and more the surest path to advancement" within the military, says John Morse, who retired as a Navy captain after twenty-eight years in the service. . . .
>
> The other path that procurement opens leads outside the military, toward the contracting firms. To know even a handful of professional soldiers above the age of forty and the rank of major is to keep hearing, in the usual catalogue of life changes, that many have resigned from the service and gone to the contractors: to Martin Marietta, Northrop, Lockheed, to the scores of consulting firms and middlemen, whose offices fill the skyscrapers of Rosslyn, Virginia, across the river from the capital. In 1959, Senator Paul Douglas of Illinois reported that 768 retired senior officers (generals, admirals, colonels, and Navy captains) worked for defense contractors. Ten years later Senator William Proxmire of Wisconsin said that the number had increased to 2,072.

Almost thirty years after those words were written, the situation has grown far worse. Until we decide (or are forced) to dismantle our empire, sell off most of our military bases in other people's countries, and bring our military expenditures into line with those of the rest of the world, we are destined to go bankrupt in the name of national defense. We are well on our way, which is why the Obama administration faces such critical—and difficult—decisions when it comes to the Pentagon budget.

PART V

HOW TO END IT

15

DISMANTLING THE EMPIRE

July 30, 2009

However ambitious President Barack Obama's domestic plans, one unacknowledged issue has the potential to destroy any reform efforts he might launch. Think of it as the eight-hundred-pound gorilla in the American living room: our long-standing reliance on imperialism and militarism in our relations with other countries and the vast, potentially ruinous global empire of bases that goes with it. The failure to begin to deal with our bloated military establishment and the profligate use of it in missions for which it is hopelessly inappropriate will, sooner rather than later, condemn the United States to a devastating trio of consequences: imperial overstretch, perpetual war, and insolvency, leading to a likely collapse similar to that of the former Soviet Union.

According to the 2008 official Pentagon inventory of our military bases around the world, our empire consists of 865 facilities in more than 40 countries and overseas U.S. territories. We deploy more than 190,000 troops in 46 countries and territories. In just one such country, Japan, at the end of March 2008, we still had 99,295 people connected to U.S. military forces living and working there—49,364 members of our armed services, 45,753 dependent family members, and 4,178 civilian employees. Some 13,975 of these were crowded into the small island of Okinawa, the largest concentration of foreign troops anywhere in Japan.

These massive concentrations of American military power outside the United States are not needed for our defense. They are, if anything, a prime contributor to our numerous conflicts with other countries. They are also unimaginably expensive. According to Anita Dancs, an analyst for the website Foreign Policy in Focus, the United States spends approximately $250 billion each year maintaining its global military presence. The sole purpose of this is to give us hegemony—that is, control or dominance— over as many nations on the planet as possible.

We are like the British at the end of World War II: desperately trying to shore up an empire that we never needed and can no longer afford, using methods that often resemble those of failed empires of the past—including the Axis powers of World War II and the former Soviet Union. There is an important lesson for us in the British decision, starting in 1945, to liquidate their empire relatively voluntarily, rather than being forced to do so by defeat in war, as were Japan and Germany, or by debilitating colonial conflicts, as were the French and Dutch. We should follow the British example. (Alas, they are currently backsliding and following our example by assisting us in the war in Afghanistan.)

Here are three basic reasons why we must liquidate our empire or else watch it liquidate us.

1. WE CAN NO LONGER AFFORD OUR POSTWAR EXPANSIONISM

Shortly after his election as president, Barack Obama, in a speech announcing several members of his new cabinet, stated as fact that "[w]e have to maintain the strongest military on the planet." A few weeks later, on March 12, 2009, in a speech at the National Defense University in Washington, D.C., the president again insisted, "Now make no mistake, this nation will maintain our military dominance. We will have the strongest armed forces in the history of the world." And in a commencement address to the cadets of the U.S. Naval Academy on May 22, Obama stressed that "[w]e will maintain America's military dominance and keep you the finest fighting force the world has ever seen."

What he failed to note is that the United States no longer has the capability to remain a global hegemon, and to pretend otherwise is to invite disaster.

According to a growing consensus of economists and political scientists around the world, it is impossible for the United States to continue in that role while emerging into full view as a crippled economic power. No such configuration has ever persisted in the history of imperialism. The University of Chicago's Robert Pape, author of the important study *Dying to Win: The Strategic Logic of Suicide Terrorism*, typically writes:

> America is in unprecedented decline. The self-inflicted wounds of the Iraq war, growing government debt, increasingly negative current-account balances and other internal economic weaknesses have cost the United States real power in today's world of rapidly spreading knowledge and technology. If present trends continue, we will look back on the Bush years as the death knell of American hegemony.

There is something absurd, even Kafkaesque, about our military empire. Jay Barr, a bankruptcy attorney, makes this point using an insightful analogy:

Whether liquidating or reorganizing, a debtor who desires bankruptcy protection must provide a list of expenses, which, if considered reasonable, are offset against income to show that only limited funds are available to repay the bankrupted creditors. Now imagine a person filing for bankruptcy claiming that he could not repay his debts because he had the astronomical expense of maintaining at least 737 facilities overseas that provide exactly zero return on the significant investment required to sustain them. . . . He could not qualify for liquidation without turning over many of his assets for the benefit of creditors, including the valuable foreign real estate on which he placed his bases.

In other words, the United States is not seriously contemplating its own bankruptcy. It is instead ignoring the meaning of its precipitate economic decline and flirting with insolvency.

Nick Turse, author of *The Complex: How the Military Invades Our Everyday Lives*, calculates that we could clear $2.6 billion if we would sell our base assets at Diego Garcia in the Indian Ocean and earn another $2.2 billion if we did the same with Guantánamo Bay in Cuba. These are only two of our more than eight hundred overblown military enclaves.

Our unwillingness to retrench, much less liquidate, represents a striking historical failure of the imagination. In his first official visit to China since becoming treasury secretary, Timothy Geithner assured an audience of students at Beijing University, "Chinese assets [invested in the United States] are very safe." According to press reports, the students responded with loud laughter. Well they might.

In May 2009, the Office of Management and Budget predicted that in 2010 the United States will be burdened with a budget deficit of at least $1.75 trillion. This includes neither a projected

$640 billion budget for the Pentagon nor the costs of waging two remarkably expensive wars. The sum is so immense that it will take several generations for American citizens to repay the costs of George W. Bush's imperial adventures—if they ever can or will. It represents about 13 percent of our current gross domestic product (that is, the value of everything we produce). It is worth noting that the target demanded of European nations wanting to join the Euro Zone is a deficit no greater than 3 percent of GDP.

Thus far, President Obama has announced measly cuts of only $8.8 billion in wasteful and worthless weapons spending, including his cancellation of the F-22 fighter aircraft. The actual Pentagon budget for next year will in fact be larger, not smaller, than the bloated final budget of the Bush era. Far bolder cuts in our military expenditures will obviously be required in the very near future if we intend to maintain any semblance of fiscal integrity.

2. WE ARE GOING TO LOSE THE WAR IN AFGHANISTAN AND IT WILL HELP BANKRUPT US

One of our major strategic blunders in Afghanistan was not to have recognized that both Great Britain and the Soviet Union attempted to pacify Afghanistan using the same military methods as ours and failed disastrously. We seem to have learned nothing from Afghanistan's modern history—to the extent that we even know what it is. Between 1849 and 1947, Britain sent almost annual expeditions against the Pashtun tribes and subtribes living in what was then called the North-West Frontier Territories—the area along either side of the artificial border between Afghanistan and Pakistan called the Durand Line. This frontier was created in 1893 by Britain's foreign secretary for India, Sir Mortimer Durand.

Neither Britain nor Pakistan has ever managed to establish

effective control over the area. As the eminent historian Louis Dupree put it in his book *Afghanistan*: "Pashtun tribes, almost genetically expert at guerrilla warfare after resisting centuries of all comers and fighting among themselves when no comers were available, plagued attempts to extend the Pax Britannica into their mountain homeland." An estimated 41 million Pashtuns live in an undemarcated area along the Durand Line and profess no loyalties to the central governments of either Pakistan or Afghanistan.

The region known today as the Federally Administered Tribal Areas (FATA) of Pakistan is administered directly by Islamabad, which—just as British imperial officials did—has divided the territory into seven agencies, each with its own "political agent" who wields much the same powers as his colonial-era predecessor. Then as now, the part of FATA known as Waziristan and the home of Pashtun tribesmen offered the fiercest resistance.

According to Paul Fitzgerald and Elizabeth Gould, experienced Afghan hands and coauthors of *Invisible History: Afghanistan's Untold Story*:

> If Washington's bureaucrats don't remember the history of the region, the Afghans do. The British used air power to bomb these same Pashtun villages after World War I and were condemned for it. When the Soviets used MiGs and the dreaded Mi-24 Hind helicopter gunships to do it during the 1980s, they were called criminals. For America to use its overwhelming firepower in the same reckless and indiscriminate manner defies the world's sense of justice and morality while turning the Afghan people and the Islamic world even further against the United States.

In 1932, in a series of Guernica-like atrocities, the British used poison gas in Waziristan. The disarmament convention of the same year sought a ban against the aerial bombardment of civilians, but as Fitzgerald and Gould note, David Lloyd George, who had been British prime minister during World War I, gloated: "We insisted on reserving the right to bomb niggers." His view prevailed.

The United States continues to act similarly, but with the new excuse that our killing of noncombatants is a result of "collateral damage," or human error. Using pilotless drones guided with only minimal accuracy from computers at military bases in the Arizona and Nevada deserts, among other places, we have killed hundreds, perhaps thousands, of unarmed bystanders in Pakistan and Afghanistan. The Pakistani and Afghan governments have repeatedly warned that we are alienating precisely the people we claim to be saving for democracy.

When in May 2009 General Stanley McChrystal was appointed as the commander in Afghanistan, he ordered new limits on air attacks, including those carried out by the CIA, except when needed to protect allied troops. Unfortunately, as if to illustrate the incompetence of our chain of command, only two days after this order, on June 23, 2009, the United States carried out a drone attack against a funeral procession that killed at least eighty people, the single deadliest U.S. attack on Pakistani soil so far. There was virtually no reporting of these developments by the mainstream American press or on the network television news. (At the time, the media were almost totally preoccupied by the sexual adventures of the governor of South Carolina and the death of pop star Michael Jackson.)

Our military operations in both Pakistan and Afghanistan have long been plagued by inadequate and inaccurate intelligence about both countries, ideological preconceptions about which parties we should support and which ones we should oppose, and myopic understandings of what we could possibly hope to achieve. Fitzgerald and Gould, for example, charge that, contrary to our own intelligence service's focus on Afghanistan, "Pakistan has always been the problem." They add:

> Pakistan's army and its Inter-Services Intelligence branch . . . from 1973 on, has played the key role in funding and directing first the *mujahideen* . . . and then the Taliban. It is Pakistan's army that controls its nuclear weapons, constrains the development of democratic institutions, trains Taliban fighters in suicide attacks and orders them to fight American and NATO soldiers protecting the Afghan government.

The Pakistani army and its intelligence arm are staffed, in part, by devout Muslims who fostered the Taliban in Afghanistan to meet the needs of their own agenda, though not necessarily to advance an Islamic jihad. Their purposes have always included keeping Afghanistan free of Russian or Indian influence, providing a training and recruiting ground for mujahideen guerrillas to be used in places such as Kashmir (fought over by both Pakistan and India), containing Islamic radicalism in Afghanistan (and so keeping it out of Pakistan), and extorting huge amounts of money from Saudi Arabia, the Persian Gulf emirates, and the United States to pay and train "freedom fighters" throughout the Islamic world. Pakistan's consistent policy has been to support the clandestine policies of the Inter-Services Intelligence and thwart the influence of its major enemy and competitor, India.

Colonel Douglas MacGregor, U.S. Army (retired), an adviser to the Center for Defense Information in Washington, summarizes our hopeless project in South Asia this way: "Nothing we do will compel 125 million Muslims in Pakistan to make common cause with a United States in league with the two states that are unambiguously anti-Muslim: Israel and India."

Obama's mid-2009 "surge" of troops into southern Afghanistan and particularly into Helmand Province, a Taliban stronghold, is fast becoming darkly reminiscent of General William Westmoreland's continuous requests in Vietnam for more troops and his promises that, if we would ratchet up the violence just a little more and tolerate a few more casualties, we would certainly break the will of the Vietnamese insurgents. This was a total misreading of the nature of the conflict in Vietnam, just as it is in Afghanistan today.

Twenty years after the forces of the Red Army withdrew from Afghanistan in disgrace, the last Russian general to command them, General Boris Gromov, issued his own prediction. Disaster, he insisted, will come to the thousands of new forces Obama is sending there, just as it did to the Soviet Union's, which lost some 15,000 soldiers in its own Afghan war. We should recognize that we are wasting time, lives, and resources in an area where we have never understood the political dynamics and continue to make the wrong choices.

3. WE NEED TO END THE SECRET SHAME OF OUR EMPIRE OF BASES

In March, *New York Times* op-ed columnist Bob Herbert noted, "Rape and other forms of sexual assault against women is the great shame of the U.S. armed forces, and there is no evidence that this ghastly problem, kept out of sight as much as possible, is diminishing." He continued:

New data released by the Pentagon showed an almost 9 percent increase in the number of sexual assaults—2,923—and a 25 percent increase in such assaults reported by women serving in Iraq and Afghanistan [over the past year]. Try to imagine how bizarre it is that women in American uniforms who are enduring all the stresses related to serving in a combat zone have to also worry about defending themselves against rapists wearing the same uniform and lining up in formation right beside them.

The problem is exacerbated by having our troops garrisoned in overseas bases located cheek by jowl next to civilian populations and often preying on them like foreign conquerors. For example, sexual violence against women and girls by American GIs has been out of control in Okinawa, Japan's poorest prefecture, ever since it was permanently occupied by our soldiers, Marines, and airmen some sixty-four years ago.

That island was the scene of the largest anti-American demonstrations since the end of World War II after the 1995 kidnapping, rape, and attempted murder of a twelve-year-old schoolgirl by two Marines and a sailor. The problem of rape has been ubiquitous around all of our bases on every continent and has probably contributed as much to our being loathed abroad as the policies of the Bush administration or our economic exploitation of poverty-stricken countries whose raw materials we covet.

The military itself has done next to nothing to protect its own female soldiers or to defend the rights of innocent bystanders forced to live next to our often racially biased and predatory troops. "The military's record of prosecuting rapists is not just lousy, it's atrocious," writes Herbert. In territories occupied by American military forces, the high command and the State Department make strenuous efforts to enact so-called Status of Forces Agreements (SOFAs) that will prevent host governments from gaining jurisdiction over our troops who commit crimes overseas. The SOFAs also make it easier for our military to spirit culprits out of a country before they can be apprehended by local authorities.

This issue was well illustrated by the case of an Australian teacher, a longtime resident of Japan, who in April 2002 was raped by a sailor from the aircraft carrier USS *Kitty Hawk*, then based at the big naval base at Yokosuka. She identified her assailant and reported him to both Japanese and U.S. authorities. Instead of his being arrested and effectively prosecuted, the victim herself was harassed and humiliated by the local Japanese police. Meanwhile, the United States discharged the suspect from the Navy but allowed him to escape Japanese law by returning him to the United States, where he lives today.

In the course of trying to obtain justice, the Australian teacher discovered that almost fifty years earlier, in October 1953, the Japanese and American governments had signed a secret "understanding" as part of their SOFA in which Japan agreed to waive its jurisdiction if the crime was not of "national importance to Japan." The United States argued strenuously for this codicil because it feared that otherwise it would face the likelihood of some 350 servicemen per year being sent to Japanese jails for sex crimes.

Since that time the United States has negotiated similar wording in SOFAs with Canada, Ireland, Italy, and Denmark. According to the *Handbook of the Law of Visiting Forces* (2001), the Japanese practice has become the norm for SOFAs throughout the world, with predictable results. In Japan, of 3,184 U.S. military personnel who committed crimes between 2001 and 2008, 83 percent were not prosecuted. In Iraq, we have signed a SOFA that bears a strong resemblance to the first postwar one we had with Japan: namely, military personnel and military contractors accused of off-duty crimes will remain in U.S. custody while Iraqis investigate. This is, of course, a perfect opportunity to spirit the culprits out of the country before they can be charged.

Within the military itself, the journalist Dahr Jamail, author of *Beyond the Green Zone: Dispatches from an Unembedded Journalist in Occupied Iraq*, speaks of the "culture of unpunished sexual assaults" and the "shockingly low numbers of courts martial" for rapes and other forms of sexual attacks. Helen Benedict, author of *The Lonely Soldier: The Private War of Women Serving in Iraq*, quotes this figure in a 2009 Pentagon report on military sexual assaults: 90 percent of the rapes in the military are never reported at all and, when they are, the consequences for the perpetrator are negligible.

It is fair to say that the U.S. military has created a worldwide sexual playground for its personnel and protected them to a large extent from the consequences of their behavior. I believe a better solution would be to radically reduce the size of our standing army and bring the troops home from countries where they do not understand their environments and have been taught to think of the inhabitants as inferior to themselves.

10 STEPS TOWARD LIQUIDATING THE EMPIRE

Dismantling the American empire would, of course, involve many steps. Here are ten key places to begin.

1. We need to put a halt to the serious environmental damage done by our bases planetwide. We also need to stop writing SOFAs that exempt us from any responsibility for cleaning up after ourselves.
2. We must end the burden of our empire of bases and of the "opportunity costs" that go with them—the things we might

otherwise do with our talents and resources but can't or won't.

3. We must end the use of torture. In the 1960s and 1970s we helped overthrow the elected governments in Brazil and Chile and underwrote regimes of torture that prefigured our own treatment of prisoners in Iraq and Afghanistan. (See, for instance, A. J. Langguth, *Hidden Terrors*, on how the United States spread torture methods to Brazil and Uruguay.) Dismantling the empire would potentially mean an end to the modern American record of using torture abroad.

4. We need to cut the ever-lengthening train of camp followers, dependents, civilian employees of the Department of Defense, and hucksters—along with their expensive medical facilities, housing requirements, swimming pools, clubs, golf courses, and so forth—that follow our military enclaves around the world.

5. We need to discredit the myth promoted by the military-industrial complex that our military establishment is valuable to us in terms of jobs, scientific research, and defense. These alleged advantages have long been discredited by serious economic research. Ending empire would make this happen.

6. As a self-respecting democratic nation, we need to stop being the world's largest exporter of arms and munitions and quit educating Third World militaries in the techniques of torture, military coups, and service as proxies for our imperialism. A prime candidate for immediate closure is the so-called School of the Americas, the U.S. Army's infamous military academy at Fort Benning, Georgia, for Latin American military officers.

7. Given the growing constraints on the federal budget, we should abolish the Reserve Officers' Training Corps and other long-standing programs that promote militarism in our schools.

8. We need to restore discipline and accountability in our armed forces by radically scaling back our reliance on civilian contractors, private military companies, and agents working for the military outside the chain of command and the Uniform Code of Military Justice. (See Jeremy Scahill, *Blackwater: The Rise of the World's Most Powerful Mercenary Army.*)

9. We need to reduce, not increase, the size of our standing army and deal much more effectively with the long-term wounds our soldiers receive and the combat stress they undergo.

10. To repeat the main message of this essay, we must give up our inappropriate reliance on military force as the chief means of attempting to achieve foreign policy objectives.

Unfortunately, few empires of the past voluntarily gave up their dominions in order to remain independent, self-governing polities. The two most important recent examples are the British and Soviet empires. If we do not learn from their examples, our decline and fall is foreordained.

NOTE ON SOURCES

All but the introduction to this book and two of the pieces in it appeared first online at the website TomDispatch.com, and there they were heavily sourced. Instead of footnotes, most had links, and, even when there were footnotes, the cites were normally largely to the URLs of various websites. A long set of URLs as footnotes in a book is, however, both awkward and largely useless. As a result, the essays in this book are unfootnoted and unsourced. However, if you go to TomDispatch.com and use either the search window or the website's month-by-month archives, you can check the original sourcing on any of these pieces. The Internet offers the first democratic form of footnoting; unfortunately—fair warning—a certain number of those links do go dead over time.

ACKNOWLEDGMENTS

I am grateful for the helpful suggestions and inspiration of several good friends and colleagues. These include Kozy Amemiya, Alfredo and Maricler Antognini, Marshall Auerback, Juan Cole, Sam Coleman, Bruce Cumings, Sandy Dijkstra, Giorgio and Noretta Freddi, Pat Hatcher, Barry Keehn, Ken Kopp, Thomas Royden, Michael Rubano, Chiho Sawada, Nick Turse, and Dustin Wright. Also, many thanks to my eagle-eyed copy editor, Emily DeHuff.

My greatest debt, however, is to my devoted publisher, Sara Bershtel of Metropolitan Books, and to my two exacting editors, Tom Engelhardt of TomDispatch.com and Sheila K. Johnson, my wife.

INDEX

ABOUT THE AUTHOR

Chalmers Johnson is the author or editor of seventeen books on subjects ranging from revolution to Chinese and Japanese politics, the high-speed growth of the East Asian economies, and his Blowback Trilogy on American imperialism and militarism. For thirty years he was a professor of international politics at the University of California, Berkeley and San Diego. From 1967 to 1973, he also served as a consultant to the Office of National Estimates of the CIA.

The American Empire Project

In an era of unprecedented military strength, leaders of the United States, the global hyperpower, have increasingly embraced imperial ambitions. How did this significant shift in purpose and policy come about? And what lies down the road?

The American Empire Project is a response to the changes that have occurred in America's strategic thinking as well as in its military and economic posture. Empire, long considered an offense against America's democratic heritage, now threatens to define the relationship between our country and the rest of the world. The American Empire Project publishes books that question this development, examine the origins of U.S. imperial aspirations, analyze their ramifications at home and abroad, and discuss alternatives to this dangerous trend.

The project was conceived by Tom Engelhardt and Steve Fraser, editors who are themselves historians and writers. Published by Metropolitan Books, an imprint of Henry Holt and Company, its titles include *Hegemony or Survival* and *Failed States* by Noam Chomsky, the Blowback Trilogy by Chalmers Johnson, *The Limits of Power* by Andrew Bacevich, *Crusade* by James Carroll, *Blood and Oil* by Michael Klare, *Dilemmas of Domination* by Walden Bello, *Devil's Game* by Robert Dreyfuss, *A Question of Torture* by Alfred McCoy, *A People's History of American Empire* by Howard Zinn, *The Complex* by Nick Turse, and *Empire's Workshop* by Greg Grandin.

For more information about the American Empire Project and for a list of forthcoming titles, please visit www.americanempire project.com.